Ball Pythons in Captivity
by Kevin McCurley

Professional Breeders Series™

E C O

© 2005 by ECO Herpetological Publishing & Distribution.

ISBN 978-0-9767334-8-x

Copies available from:

ECO Herpetological Publishing & Distribution
915 Seymour Ave. Lansing, MI 48906 USA
telephone: 517.487.5595   fax: 517.371.2709
email: ecoorders@hotmail.com website: http://www.reptileshirts.com

T-Rex Products, Inc.
http://t-rexproducts.com

Zoo Book Sales
http://www.zoobooksales.com

LIVING ART publishing
http://www.livingartpublishing.com

Design and layout by Russ Gurley.
Cover design by Rafael Porrata.
Printed in China

Front Cover: An incredible Hypomelanistic Mojave Ball Python. Photo by Dan Sutherland of The Snake Keeper.
Back Cover: Coral Bumblebee Ball Python. Photo by Kevin McCurley of NERD.

ACKNOWLEDGEMENTS

Everyday there is more of "us" and "our world", every day there is less of the natural world. Learn to appreciate life before it appears as a memory in a Zoo or a book.

I wish to thank my Dad, Ellis McCurley. He took me seriously from my twelve-year-old birthday wish: "I think the best birthday present would be a Boa constrictor!" So he took me shopping and bought me a dress!! No, not really! He made me read and educate myself before I was ready to have a pet snake. Who would have thought where it would lead?

Thanks to my mom for letting me bring my first snakes into her household. She tolerated my hobby and eventually accepted it as part of who I am.

Thanks to Kara Glasgow, who pained through editing my long rants and raw manuscripts for the book. Her knowledge of reptiles proved invaluable as she helped to clarify and organize my thoughts.

Thank you to the breeders, keepers and everyone that submitted photos for this book. In some cases I was not able to use the pictures because of people using their "Snoopy's First Camera" and some strange poses, but many awesome shots made it in and you will see them here.

Thanks to the Ball Python Breeders – that continue to make me jealous with their collections and new mutations. There are some killer collections showing us that the sky is the limit. You keep me going in my pursuit of creating something new and exciting.

To anyone that I left out - and I am sure I have missed a few - I apologize. Know that you are appreciated and this is the exact weapon you need to bust on me next time you see me!

Kevin McCurley
NERD

TABLE OF CONTENTS

Albino
Albino Clown
Butter
Caramel Glow
Clown
Pastel Clown
Coral Glow
Desert Ghost
Ghost
Lavender Albino
Blue-eyed Leucistic
Lemon Pastel - Super
Pied
Pinstripe
Spider
Ghost Spider
Lemon Bumblebee
Killer Bee

Chapter 1. The Ball Python in Nature

Natural History

Scientific Name / Classification

Along with boas and the other python species, ball pythons are members of the taxonomic family Boidae. The ball python's Latin name is *Python regius*, which translates to "royal python," and it is often referred to as such throughout Europe and countries outside of the United States. This species has earned the name "ball python" through its defensive behavior of coiling its body into a protective ball around the head when frightened. In captivity, some shy animals may exhibit this technique and remain tightly coiled into a ball while being handled, and only uncoil after handling.

Habitat

This smallest of the African python species ranges from West and Central Africa in the countries of Nigeria, Uganda, Liberia, Sierra Leone, and Guinea. The majority of ball pythons imported into the

Open savannah a chief part of the habitat of the ball python, *Python regius*. Photo by Stefan Broghammer.

1

U.S. originate from Benin, Ghana, and Togo. They exist in tropical arid conditions and live within temperature extremes of 60° to 110° F. Much of the animal's life is spent underground in vacant or active rodent burrow systems, and foraging and movement occurs only after nightfall. They generally inhabit open savannah and areas with sparse forest growth. This python does well in farmed areas where rodent populations are high and water is available. Farming in some cases has proven beneficial to ball python numbers, allowing higher population levels than a savannah condition would normally support. Ball pythons are a farmer's best friend as they can help contain rodent populations that compete for the farmer's crops. Unfortunately many African farmers are terrified of snakes and many ball pythons are killed regardless of their benefit.

Size

Ball pythons are robust and heavy-bodied. The head is well-defined and broad, with a distinctly rounded snout, and the neck is fairly thin and easily discernible from the rest of the body and head. Average adult size for this species is 36" to 48" and females are generally

A large adult female ball python and a neonate.

An assortment of ball pythons from newly hatched to adult.

larger than males. Average hatchling size is between 8" to 12".
While record size for the ball python is reportedly 7.5', specimens
over 5' are considered large and animals over 6' in length are rarely
encountered. The largest animal I have personally known
was an old imported female that weighed in at nine pounds.

Lifespan

Average lifespan of the captive ball python is approximately 20 years,
although a 35-year plus lifespan would seem reasonable with proper
care. The species longevity record is reportedly 48 years for a
captive zoo specimen (Slavens, pers. com). We have a documented
record of a 40 + year old female laying nine viable eggs in 2005
(Steve Michaelson, pers. com.).

Chapter 2. Ball Pythons in Captivity

A 10-gallon terrarium can be a suitable enclosure for a baby or juvenile ball python.

Ball Pythons as Pets

Ball pythons make excellent pets due to their small size and ease of keeping. They are typically gentle animals that often seem to enjoy being handled and interacting with the keeper. Their care is far less demanding than conventional pets such as cats or dogs. Feeding does not require a rigorous schedule that most house pets need, and vacations will do little to affect the quality of care. Snakes can go weeks with little care as long as fresh water is available. They are very clean, secretive, and do not make noise. They do not require veterinarian check ups or routine worming. They, other than wild caught imports, make for an ideal beginner snake and prove suitable for children who are supervised in handling and are taught basic care. Unlike corn snakes and kingsnakes, which may be a bit small and easily lost by children, ball pythons are slow moving and easy to handle. In addition, they are inexpensive to maintain, hardy, and long lived.

Caging Requirements

The ball python is obviously not a "typical" household pet. In other words, it is not a domestic animal that can easily adapt to the fluctuations in temperature and humidity that the average household undergoes on a regular basis.

All reptiles are ectothermic (cold blooded), and unable to internally regulate their body temperature. They depend on environmental conditions to meet their needs for both cool and warm temperatures. Unlike a dog or cat that would remain largely unaffected by a 10-degree temperature hike or a 20% drop in humidity, reptiles are extremely sensitive to such changes. In some cases, changes in the environment act as "triggers" to let a snake know it's time to eat more or eat less, or to search out a mate for breeding purposes. When environmental triggers occur at the right time, they can be used by the herpetoculturist to induce desired results – i.e. breeding or feeding. However, if a pet ball python is kept in an uncontrolled environment, these continuous and sometimes rapid changes may cause the animal to become stressed, to quit eating, and even to develop an illness or medical condition as a result of that stress. **It is the snake owner's responsibility to thoroughly understand the python's needs and to meet them as best as possible by creating the correct captive environment.**

It is highly recommended that the herpetoculturist purchase and assemble an appropriate enclosure prior to acquiring the snake, regardless of whether this is the first snake or the fiftieth. Having a proper enclosure set up with temperature and humidity levels established will provide the snake with a smooth transition into its new home.

Cage Size

Adult ball pythons require cage dimensions of approximately 36" long by 18" wide, or 24" long x 12" wide for subadult animals. Hatchling ball pythons tend to thrive in a much smaller enclosure, approximately 5" wide and 10" long. Large spacious cages may be too overwhelming for a small snake, and as a result may cause the animal to stress and to quit feeding. It's important to keep in mind

A 20-gallon long terrarium is a suitable enclosure for a juvenile to adult ball python.

that a baby python is at the "bottom of the food chain," and programmed by nature to be very secretive in order to survive. Providing a hatchling or young ball python with hiding areas (see Hide Box on pg. 25) that clutter the cage will often allow this animal to feel secure, as this type of habitat appeals to its secretive ways. A baby can do well in a 10 to 20 gallon size cage. The cage should always be large enough to provide the ball python with a distinct warm side and cool side (with the exception of babies being housed in plastic shoeboxes at a moderate ambient temperature).

Cage Type

There are a wide variety of caging options available to the ball python keeper. Regardless of the type of enclosure used, it must be capable of providing the correct environment for the snake, and must be completely secure and escape-proof. Snakes are natural escape artists that can disappear from a cage very quickly if allowed the chance to do so. The cage must be easy to lock or keep securely closed; when the animal learns an escape technique you can count on the fact it will do it again if given the chance. Once outside of the cage, escaped snakes often find themselves in a world where their needs are not met, and unless recovered quickly, a loose ball python may fail to survive in a new and potentially hostile environment.

Let's take a moment to review some of the caging options available to keep a ball python safe and sound.

Glass Tank / Aquarium

Glass tanks are probably the most widely used type of snake enclosure, especially among keepers with one or just a few snakes. This type of enclosure is available at pet stores or reptile expos. Many keepers like the high-visibility aspect of glass and enjoy creating pleasing natural displays within the vivariums. Glass tanks are also fairly inexpensive compared to some other types of caging and they can be easily cleaned and disinfected. A popular glass cage readily available in most pet and specialty stores is the *Critter Cage®* from All-Glass. This enclosure features a sliding screen top with an attachment that can accommodate a pin style lock or even a small padlock if necessary. These tops are a good choice when dealing with pet snakes in a household with small children to prevent any accidental and unsupervised interaction.

Screen tops are typically utilized with glass enclosures and provide excellent ventilation and airflow. By the same token this combination can make it difficult to maintain the correct environment for the inhabitant of the tank – in this case your ball python. A screen top allows for a constant exchange between the conditions of the snake's tank and the conditions of the room in which the tank is kept. This can mean necessary heat and humidity escaping the ball python's environment and potential subopti-

A complete ball python cage - a 40-gallon *Critter Cage*® with locking lid.

mum temperatures and conditions within the tank. Many keepers have successfully eliminated this issue by placing a piece of Plexiglas over the screen top, or even wrapping a portion of the screen in cellophane to prevent heat and humidity loss.

Another factor to keep in mind when using glass tanks is the ball python's shy demeanor. Sometimes the great visibility offered by these tanks is overwhelming and stressful to the inhabitant. Utilizing hide boxes (multiple if necessary) within a glass enclosure will give the ball python an opportunity to hide if it feels threatened. Always provide a choice of hide locations within a glass vivarium, one in a warmer heated end and another in the cooler end.

Plastic Herp Caging

Due to the rapid rate at which herpetoculture has grown as a hobby over the past decade, a plethora of reptile-specific products have been created and made available to the private sector. Among these products are some quality cages specifically designed for keeping reptiles. Plastic has become a popular cage material among snake keepers for several reasons: It's easy to heat, easy to disinfect, doesn't warp under humid conditions, it's mite-resistant, it's light-weight, and the cages are often stackable. Pre-made plastic enclosures come in a selection of colors, sizes, and price ranges, and quite a few manufacturers offer custom options like vents or built-in lighting and heating. Since they're made expressly for reptile keeping, these cages tend to allow for more precise environmental control than glass or wooden enclosures. As with any enclosure, plastic caging should be escape-proof, and even lockable if necessary to keep small children out and to keep snakes in.

Rack System

Rack systems allow the herpetoculturist to maintain larger numbers of snakes in a more space-efficient manner. The concept of a rack system is very simple: Multiple levels of shelves containing a number of individual snake boxes. Think of it as a chest of drawers made for keeping snakes. Racks are available in a range of materials, the most

Zoo Products PVC caging.

common being plastic, metal, and wood. Plastic storage boxes (i.e. Rubbermaid® and Sterilite®) are frequently used in these racks to house individual snakes, although some rack manufacturers offer boxes specifically created for their rack systems. Snake racks often have some sort of heating element incorporated into the design – typically heat tape or heat cable located at one side of the rack to provide a thermal gradient.

Rack heating elements should **always** be used in conjunction with a thermostat or other heat-controlling device. Certain rack styles feature "open air" construction, similar to a screen top, which can help prevent overheating and provide excellent ventilation. For racks utilizing "closed construc-tion" design, the snake keeper must take care to ensure that each snake box is sufficiently venti-lated to provide proper air flow.

The majority of commer-cial breeders use Free-dom Breeder rack systems to house and breed ball

The Animal Plastics shoe box rack system provides housing for multiple baby snakes.

pythons. This rack system is an excellent way to manage any number of snakes. This type of caging allows the snake to remain secretive and provides the right environment. They also make excellent rodent breeding racks in which quantities of rodents can be produced with minimal time and effort. For more information, see http://www.freedombreeder.com.

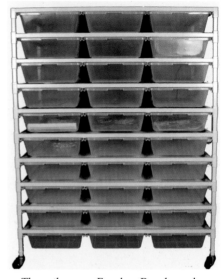

The author uses Freedom Breeder rack systems for all of his ball pythons.

Plastic Storage Boxes

The plastic storage box is the predecessor to the rack system. Snake keepers have used these boxes for years for housing everything from hatchling to adult ball pythons, not to mention many other species. Plastic storage boxes are very inexpensive, easily disinfected, lightweight, and with a little ingenuity can be set up to provide the correct temperature and humidity conditions required to keep a ball python healthy. It is important to note that plastic storage boxes often do not have securely locking lids; modifications must be made to ensure that any snake kept in one cannot escape. Additionally, ventilation must often be added to storage box enclosures.

This can easily be done by melting a number of holes in each side of

A plastic shoe box can provide a simple but functional enclosure for a young ball python.

Zoo Products' PVC cage systems provide an attractive, clean, and long-lasting cage.

the box using a soldering iron. If the box appears wet inside from condensation when a heat source is applied under the container, it needs more ventilation.

Wood and Melamine Caging

Many reptile keepers use enclosures constructed of wood or melamine (laminated particleboard). Some of these cages are furniture-quality pieces and can make excellent displays. On the other hand, if not properly sealed wood can be extremely difficult to disinfect due to its porous nature, and may harbor bacteria and fungi. Unfinished wood as a cage material is a short-term solution and should not be considered for long-term use. It will absorb moisture and urine, and warp unless it is properly sealed.

IMPORTANT

Do not house ball pythons in wire or fabric mesh / screen cages. Enclosures of this type are not capable of retaining the heat and humidity necessary to provide a suitable environment for a ball python.

Heating and Heat Control

Ball pythons, like all other snakes, are ectothermic. This means they must seek out external heat sources to maintain the body temperatures needed for general health, as well as for activities such as digestion of prey. Ball pythons thrive at ambient temperatures of 80 to 85° F during the day, and will tolerate 78 to 80° F at night. Additionally, ball pythons will utilize a basking area of 88 to 95° F, which should cover one-quarter to one-third of the enclosure. Providing both a warm end and cool end of the enclosure gives a ball python a thermal gradient, and allows the snake to choose the temperature at which it is most comfortable. Always ensure that there is enough room in a ball python's enclosure to allow the snake to move away from a heat source.

Temperature Tips:

Use a thermostat (more on these in a moment) to help maintain precise basking temperatures. This tool optimally allows you to create and to control your animal's microclimate.

Don't let temperatures rise or fall too sharply after your snake has eaten. Once food has been ingested the animal requires an external heat source to aid in the digestion process. If the cage temperatures sharply rise or fall this may affect the digestion of the prey item. Always know your temperatures. Correct temperatures are not a guessing game. A stick-on thermometer located on the side of the enclosure tells the temperature of the side of the enclosure, not the temperature where the snake is sitting. You should know the temperature of the basking spot. An infrared heat gun is a fancy piece of equipment that detects surface temperatures of any object. With a heat gun a keeper can read exact temperatures in the enclosure and the temperature of the snake itself at a glance.

Pay attention to the ambient (background) temperature in your snake's cage. Most household room temperatures are lower than what ball pythons need to thrive, so be prepared to compensate accordingly, i.e. adding a small space heater, keeping your snake in a warmer part of the house, having a dedicated "snake room," etc.

Heating Methods

Heat Pads / Under-Tank Heaters

Heating pads, or under-tank heaters as they are commonly known, are one of the best and most widely used methods for heating snake enclosures. A heating pad is placed under-neath one end of the snake's enclosure to provide a basking spot by warming the substrate. If using a heating pad, it should always be positioned outside of the cage to prevent the snake from burning itself in the event

Excellent and reliable undertank heating sources.

that the pad becomes too warm. Locating most heating pads within a cage can lead to electrocution, fire, and other possible hazards, please avoid this method. Always leave sufficient air space between the heating pad and a solid surface. This can be accomplished by placing small spacers or rubber "feet" at each corner of your snake's enclosure. It is always wise to use a thermostat or rheostat in conjunction with a heating pad for precise temperature control.

Special Note: Do not undersize your heating pad. Small heating pads will not efficiently create a warm basking area.

Heat Tape

Heat tape is a thin, electrical heating element encased in polyurethane. Available in 3", 4", and 11" widths, heat tape can be cut to a length that

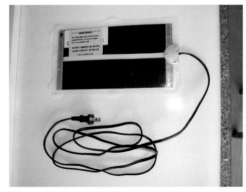

The pad is secured to the outside of the cage bottom to transfer heat into the cage.

will fit any enclosure.
Heat tape is wired by the
user, and it is highly
recommended that
anyone wishing to
attempt this process for
the first time seek the
help of an experienced
fellow reptile keeper that
has previously wired heat
tape with good results.
As with heating pads, it
is vital not to sandwich

There is a wide range of heat-emitting bulbs on the market.

heat tape between two solid surfaces. It is also very important to use a thermostat, rheostat, or other temperature controller with heat tape to avoid overheating.

Light Bulbs

Basking lights are often used by first-time snake keepers to provide a hot spot for their ball pythons, often in conjunction with a heating pad. If using a basking light to provide heat, it is important to provide a light cycle for your snake of approximately 8-12 hours. Using a timer will make this an automatic process. A heating pad will provide supplemental heat while the light bulb is turned off at night. Since light bulbs have a tendency to dry the air within a cage, providing your ball python with a humid hide (see section on humidity) will help counteract the drying effect of the bulb. Also, never use a standard spotlight bulb for a basking spot, as these bulbs focus an intense amount of light and heat in a small area and can cause serious thermal burns to a snake. Small floodlight style R30 bulbs are the best choice. I have used T-REX and Zoo Med bulbs with good success. Take into consideration the size of your snake and enclosure when choosing a basking bulb; a hatchling ball python can easily become overwhelmed by a 150-watt bulb, while a larger animal will reap little benefit from a 40-watt heat lamp. The negatives of a high- watt basking light as a heat source are obvious: It will create difficulties when controlling humidity and it may disturb a shy nocturnal animal enough that it may fail to thrive. Low wattage (25 – 60 watt) bulbs in conjunction with an under-tank heating pad will provide a distinct photoperiod and will aid in providing proper temperatures without a Sahara Desert effect. I have seen ball pythons with upper respiratory infections and massive stuck sheds due to the keeper using a high wattage light bulb and maintaining low humidity due to the cage placement in a cold room.

Take into consideration the size of your snake and enclosure when choosing a basking bulb.

Radiant Heat Panels

The radiant heat panel is comprised of a heating element enclosed in a rectangular frame, with a surface material similar to that of a drop-ceiling tile. Radiant heat panels are designed for permanent installation to the ceiling of a cage, and create a basking spot by directing heat downward. Heat panels do not emit light, nor do they typically become excessively hot to the touch. As with any heating element, it is strongly recommended that you control a heat panel with a thermostat or rheostat as an extra safety precaution.

Thermometers

One of the biggest "must have" tools for monitoring your ball python's environment is a good thermometer. Without one (if not two), it is impossible for the keeper to know how precise the temperatures are within the snake's enclosure. Two thermometers are recommended so it is easy to determine temperatures in both the warm and cool end of the cage.

There are many good thermometers available to the ball python owner, from simple analog style to high-tech infrared temp guns. No matter what, it is important to have the ability to accurately read temperatures at any time, so that corrections may be made if necessary.

Analog Thermometers

Analog thermometers are very simple, easy to use, and extremely inexpensive. Many now come with a built-in humidity gauge. To monitor temperatures, place an analog thermometer at each end of your ball python's cage. Some thermometers have suction cups or Velcro to make it easy to attach them to the interior of the enclosure.

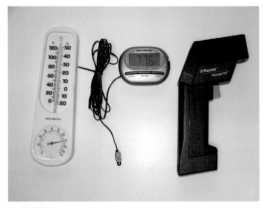

Reliable temperature monitoring is important From left to right: Analog, digital indoor/outdoor, and digital temp gun thermometers.

Digital

Digital indoor / outdoor thermometers with a remote sensor are extremely popular for their ability to read the temperature in two different locations at once. To use, simply place the thermometer at one end of the snake's cage (most have adhesive or Velcro for this purpose) and the sensor probe at the other end. Ensure that both the thermometer and probe are secure and cannot be moved around by your ball python. Remember to replace the battery as necessary. Digital thermometers are available through many herp supply companies, garden centers, and discount department stores.

Temp Gun

The "Rolls Royce" of thermometers, temp guns are favored by hobbyists and pros alike for their ability to point and shoot temperatures at any location. Whether determining the basking spot or recording the temperature of freshly-laid eggs, this tool allows the herpetoculturist to monitor warmth (or the lack thereof) throughout a snake's enclosure, or snake room for that matter. Temp guns are available in simple, stripped-down versions that give basic

A digital indoor/outdoor thermometer with a probe in a simple cage setup.

temperature readings, or can be purchased with laser sighting, minimum/maximum temperature memory, and fancy backlighting. Any of the above work equally well for the intended application. The temp gun is a must-have tool for the "Reptile Geek!"

Note: Small aquarium-style "sticker" thermometers do not always give the accurate readings necessary for properly maintaining temperatures in your snake's enclosure. They aid in monitoring the temperature of the surface on which they are located. Using multiple thermometers is the correct choice, one to monitor ambient cool end temperatures and a high range thermometer temporarily placed on or near the heat source.

Heat Control and Monitoring Methods

By this point you're aware of the importance of creating a consistently correct environment within your ball python's enclosure. Fortunately there are a variety of tools available.

Thermostats

The thermostat is an invaluable piece of equipment that can take a lot of guesswork out of maintaining proper temperatures. It monitors a heat source's output and provides power to the heat source thus providing a temperature range that the user can control. It consists of a power cord, control module for setting the desired temperature,

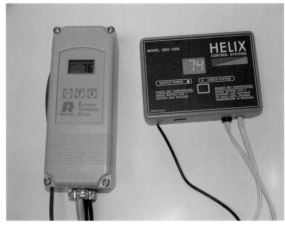

Popular on/off and pulse-proportional thermostats.

a power receptacle for connecting a heating element, and a remote thermometer/sensor probe for reading temperature levels from the heat source.

When setting up a thermostat, **it is critical to affix the temperature probe in such a way that it cannot be dislocated from the heat source.** Failure to take this precaution could result in extreme overheating. For example, if the thermostat probe fell out of the cage and onto the floor it would read the room temperature rather than the heating element temperature, and cause the heating element to run full throttle. This in turn would raise enclosure temperatures to potentially fatal levels. Many snake keepers have experienced the shock of dead and/or neurologically damaged animals due to overheating.

There are two types of thermostats available for heat control: on/off and proportional. On/off thermostats do exactly that – turn the heat source on and off to maintain the desired temperature. When the probe reads temperatures above the level set on the control module, the thermostat shuts off power to the heat source. When the temperatures drop below the desired level, the thermostat turns the power back on. Proportional thermostats simply increase and decrease the power supply as necessary to achieve the same effect, rather than completely turning the power off and on. This dimming effect is less destructive to the element when using light bulbs as a heat source. Both types of thermostats are widely used throughout herpetoculture and are very effective for temperature control when properly used.

Note: On/off thermostats are less recommended for use with light bulbs. The constant on/off flickering of the light bulb not only decreases its lifespan, but can also cause stress to the cage inhabitant.

Rheostats / Dimmers

Rheostats and dimmers provide another option for heat control. Most are simple "plug-and-play" devices that connect to a heat source via a power receptacle and plug into a wall socket. Turning a dial on the rheostat/dimmer controls power to the heat source and acts as a current (power) choke. If room temperatures vary the heat source will remain unregulated and add heat to the existing ambient temperatures. Rheostats/dimmers do not offer the precise control of a thermostat, and it is important to pay attention to temperature levels and regularly compensate accordingly for warmer or cooler conditions. Note: If ambient temperatures are 75° F and the rheostat allows a heat source to add 20° F, the hot spot in theory would be around 95° F which is good. If ambient temperatures change and become higher such as 85° F, the heat source adds another 20° F and the hot spot is now 105° F which is too hot for the snake. Rheostats and dimmers do not regulate themselves as a thermostat does!

Light

Ball pythons do not need supplemental lighting and do quite well with simple ambient light from a nearby window. If a basking light is used, it should run on a 12/12 cycle (12 hours on and 12 hours off). Continuous bright, overhead lighting is stressful to snakes, especially to a nocturnal serpent such as the ball python. Lighting left on continuously does not allow the animal its normal activity period.

Nocturnal animals typically forage and are active after sundown and before sunrise. They will hide and sleep during the day, awaiting a nighttime temperature drop and the shroud of darkness to aid in their secretive lives. Full spectrum fluorescent lights are not required but can aid in the creation of a light cycle and will better display the snake's natural colors. Provide a nightly activity period by turning off cage lighting; the use of a commercial timer makes this task simple. Many snakes will refuse to feed until the lights go out; often an animal will become active within the first few hours of nightfall. This is also an optimal period to try feeding a shy snake.

Water

Your ball python should always have access to fresh, clean water. The size and style of the water dish is up to you. If it is large enough for the python to crawl into and soak, sooner or later your snake will make the most of the opportunity, and most seem to enjoy a nice soak from time to time. Ensure that the bowl is not too deep for juvenile animals - 1" or so will suffice. Snakes of many species will occasionally defecate in their water bowls, so be prepared for cleaning, disinfecting, and a water change when necessary. It is often beneficial to have a spare water bowl for such occasions, so that one may be used as a replacement while the other is being cleaned.

Substrate

Always utilize some type of substrate (bedding) within your ball python's enclosure.

Newspaper is widely used, inexpensive, and while not always aesthetically pleasing, easy to obtain and replace.

Wood fiber beddings such as cypress mulch and shredded aspen are also very popular. Cypress mulch retains humidity well, however it is

Provide a water container large enough for the snake to immerse its entire body.

important to remember that cypress trees are not commercially grown for the purpose of mulch, and continued harvesting of these trees contributes to habitat destruction.

Aspen bedding and recycled newspaper bedding should generally be used in well-ventilated enclosures, as it has a tendency to mold when excessively wet. Always replace any soggy bedding.

Sani-Chips® bedding which is small fine chips of wood have also been used with success but I am unfamiliar with its long-term results.

Shredded coconut husk is a popular and relatively new bedding. This bedding is sold in compressed bricks that expand and yield a high capacity of bedding when mixed with water. It is fairly absorbent and widely available. I feel that this type of bedding is best blended with sand. This type of bedding is more messy than some others and may not be the best choice.

Less exciting and not recommended: Pine shavings are sometimes used, however, some snakes find the oils in pine to be irritating and the shavings tend to be dusty. Fir bark is widely sold as reptile

21

bedding. This substrate is comprised of small chunks of bark that may pose a danger if ingested.

Additionally, the large pieces are not as absorbent as other

From left to right: Bedding - cocoa peat, aspen, and finely milled cypress mulch.

substrates. Pine bark nuggets are sometimes used but are viewed unsuitable since it is often unsanitary, non-absorbent, and best left for landscaping. Reptile carpet/Astroturf is another option, but some types may be abrasive to overly active pythons, and do not always absorb urates well.

Do not use bedding that contains cedar - the oils in cedar are TOXIC to reptiles.

Avoid mulches that have been treated with pesticides, weed killers, or other chemicals.

Avoid substrates that are dusty, moldy, or contain bugs.

Routinely change substrate and provide a clean environment. This helps to ensure the health of your animal.

Humidity

Wild ball pythons spend much of their life underground in rodent burrows. The moist earth creates constant relative humidity and makes for a comfortable python. Every time the snake exhales it loses a little bit of moisture, which can ultimately contribute to dehydration, especially if the ball python is kept in a dry, sub-optimum environment. Retained (or "stuck") sheds are the first clue that a python's cage is too dry. Eventually, being kept in too dry a state will stress a ball python, potentially to the point of illness. Hatchlings are more prone to suffering from this condition.

Providing proper humidity for a ball python is important, but know that too much humidity can be as problematic as too little. First off, let's establish "humidity" as the amount of moisture in the air. Remember that warm air holds more moisture than cold air, so keep an eye on those ambient temperatures. Since relative humidity in the average household may fluctuate from 15% - 60% at various times of the year, creating a consistent humidity level for your ball python may require a little attention to detail.

To provide your snake with extra humidity, you have a couple of options:

1. Make a "humidity box" for your snake. This consists of packing a plastic container with damp sphagnum moss (think well-wrung-out wash cloth to gauge moisture), cutting a hole in the top or side and placing it in the warm end of your python's enclosure so that the

Damp sphagnum moss makes an excellent humid hide for a ball python.

snake can access the box as it pleases. This has the added benefit of providing another hiding spot for your snake, which can help it feel more secure within the enclosure. This simple tool can fix a dry shed, alleviate a respiratory infection, and create a feeding response in many situations.

2. Use cypress mulch or a similar substrate that can be misted and is mold-resistant. Cypress is good for this as it turns a tan color when dry and a rich brown when wet, giving a visual cue as to when it needs to be dampened again. If humidity is a problem, use a deep layer of cypress to hold in moisture and water it as needed. This bedding breathes and provides a simple means to proper humidity.

Hide Box

One cage accessory that is beneficial to a happy ball python is a good hide box . . . maybe even a couple of them. These are secretive snakes that appreciate and utilize a hide spot. Provide one on each end of your python's enclosure so that it doesn't have to choose between temperature and security. Clay flower pots, plastic

A secretive ball python is a happy ball python.

flowerpot trays, and commercially available specialized plastic and epoxy hide boxes all work quite well. As with any cage accessory, the hide boxes should be easy to disinfect. Hides made of wood or cork can be difficult to clean and may harbor fungus and/or bacteria.

Natural type hides (above) and utilitarian (below) hide boxes are widely available.

Hide boxes are intended to be tight, secure little nooks and crannies that make your snake feel even more secure within the main enclosure. A big, roomy hide defeats the purpose – snakes want to cram themselves into a small, enclosed space that doesn't allow easy access from potential threats. Hide boxes with one opening are often more effective than the "half log" style hides that are widely available.

If a ball python appears restless and unhappy with hiding arrangements, crumpled newspaper may create the additional security and crowded conditions the animal needs. This trick may also help when a reluctant feeder is encountered.

Natural Vivaria

Lush, planted vivaria with gentle mists and waterfalls sound great in theory, but may often fall short of a keeper's expectations. With its

A naturalistic vivarium creates a comfortable environment for the snake and a visually appealing setup for the keeper.

heavy body and nocturnally active nature, a ball python can turn a beautifully planted tank into the aftermath of "Godzilla in Tokyo" by the time you wake up the next morning.

Careful thought must be given when placing the plants and dirt. It is often better to leave plants potted and the dirt protected if possible.

Ball pythons are very curious and will find their way into the smallest nooks and crannies to explore the ultimate hiding spot. Whenever you mix dirt and water you will get mud. Keep this in mind as you attempt to plant the enclosure. Planted vivariums can be difficult to manage and to keep clean from a husbandry standpoint, and require diligent maintenance to avoid rampant bacterial and fungus growth.

None of this is said to discourage those who have the time to provide a ball python with a large, naturalistic enclosure. Setting up a planted cage is a relaxing hobby for those who enjoy it, and the reward of experiencing a wide range of the snake's natural behavior can outweigh the care and maintenance involved.

Cleaning and Maintenance

As with any animal, providing a clean environment for your ball python will help to keep it healthy and comfortable under your care. If possible double up on cage accessories such as hide

L-R: Bleach, Alphazyme Plus, Nolvasan, glass cleaner, citrus-based de-greaser.

boxes and water bowls so that you have a spare to switch out while you clean soiled cage items. Check water bowls frequently for bacterial buildup, which will manifest as a slick, slimy feeling inside the bowl. Depending on the substrate you use, either spot-clean soiled areas of the cage daily (i.e. as with aspen or mulch), or replace the substrate completely when dirty (newspaper or paper towels). With wood fiber substrates it is possible to spot-clean as you go, however don't let this method transform into a lazy husbandry habit. It is still important to pay attention to the overall substrate condition and completely change out your snake's bedding if it becomes musty, moldy, damp, or extremely dirty. Also take note of the bedding's odor; substrate with a strong ammonia smell should be changed immediately. When using wood fiber beddings, be prepared to completely change the substrate every 45-60 days, or sooner if necessary.

Thoroughly wash your ball python's enclosure with a 10% bleach/ water solution (or strong enough to smell the bleach, but not strong enough to burn your eyes), or other disinfectant such as Nolvasan® or Quatricide®, whenever you change out the bedding in the cage, whether once a week or once a month.

Make sure you rinse the cage with clean water and allow it to dry before returning the snake (having a spare, secure holding tub for the snake comes in handy here). In the interim, wash your snake's water bowl, hide boxes, and other cage accessories in a disinfectant solution at least once a week to prevent bacteria or fungi from developing.

Disinfecting solutions – Chlorhexidine (Brand name Nolvasan®), Quaternary ammonia compounds (Brand name Quatricide®), or a simple 10% bleach/water solution all make excellent agents for disinfecting cages, water bowls, hides, tools, and other equipment.

Remember that reptiles are naturally clean animals that we have transplanted into smaller quarters. It is your responsibility to keep up with your cage. Developing and practicing sound husbandry habits will not only improve your snake's quality of life, but also help you become a better keeper. By knowing what is consistently "normal" for your snake and its environment, you'll be able to pinpoint when something is off, or if an incident deserves special attention, whether a stuck shed, refused meal, or more.

Escapees

Snakes are natural escape artists, if they find an opportunity to expand their horizons they will. They have the uncanny ability to notice when you have failed to close their cage correctly or have a flaw in cage security. Once out they can go anywhere as they investigate an unfamiliar world. Many snakes are lost this way, never to be seen again. They often locate a passage into walls or under floors where they will hide and possibly become trapped. Some snakes may just wander a short distance and find a warm, quiet, safe and dark area in which to curl up and hide. They will often be more active at night and potentially wander greater distances during this period than daytime escapees.

It is critical that immediate time is taken to scan the immediate area for the inmate before it has time to really get lost. When a snake escapes it can quickly find a life-threatening situation such as cold, heat, dehydration, and injury. This new freedom does not make for the ultimate snake experience and may be a source of great frustration for the keeper. Once the snake has been out for a few days it may have located a safe place to hide and may only wander from this spot at night as it hunts and looks for water. This is a good time to look for it with a flashlight a few hours after dark.

Chapter 3. Feeding

Ball pythons are predators that require whole animal prey, usually in the form of rodents. If you have qualms about feeding rodents to your pet ball python, this is something to seriously consider **before** you acquire one. Ball pythons thrive on rodent prey, and most will eat mice and rats throughout the course of their lifetime.

Constriction

Ball pythons – like all other pythons – are constrictors, using this method to procure and subdue their prey. A ball python will strike at a prey item (a rodent in this case) and grasp it firmly, utilizing small, backward-pointing teeth to secure it. The snake will then coil around its prey and wait for the rodent to exhale. Each time the rodent exhales the python will further tighten its grip, preventing the rodent from inhaling again. Within a short period of time the rodent will lose consciousness due to lack of oxygen and expire. Once the rodent is dead, the ball python will consume the prey whole, usually (but not always) starting at the head of the rodent, and slowly swallowing the entire body. Ball pythons

A perfect match.

have very elastic skin, and the front of the jawbone is connected with a ligament instead of being solidly fused as in mammals. These characteristics assist the python in swallowing larger prey items. Caution to the first time ball python owner! The feeding response strike of a ball python is extremely and almost unbelievably fast. Care must be taken when introducing food items, as bites can occur on the hands intending to feed the snake.

Type of Prey

Ball pythons can – and typically do – eat mice and rats their entire lives. Hatchling ball pythons are often started on "hopper" mice (small, almost-weaned mice that hop around a lot, hence the name) and quickly graduate to adult mice. A baby python may require the movement of a hopper mouse to excite it and convince the animal it should be eaten. Do not feed ball pythons pink (newborn) mice, as they are a small, insufficient prey item that may fail to trigger a feeding response. As the ball python grows, most keepers choose to switch their snakes to rats, often due to the fact that it is simpler and more cost-effective to feed a snake one larger rat as opposed to many mice at a time.

A good rule of thumb for determining prey size is to "go by the girth". In other words, feed prey items only slightly larger around than your ball python. An appropriately sized prey item should leave a modestly perceptible bulge in the snake, and not make it look like the snake just ate a football.

When acquiring your ball python, speak to the person from whom you are purchasing it and find out what the snake is currently eating on a regular basis. Some keepers choose to feed their snakes chicks or quail and others will feed gerbils or hamsters.

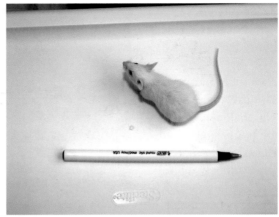

Correct size of prey for a baby ball python - Use smaller jumper mice for the first few meals.

It is strongly recommended that ball python keepers consistently offer their snakes mice or rats. Sometimes a ball python may develop a "taste" for other prey (i.e. a gerbil or chick), and it can be extremely difficult to convert the snake back onto its regular diet of mice or rats. Chicks may lack many of the nutrients a rodent has and it is better to avoid them as a food source.

Frequency

Ball pythons do well on a weekly feeding schedule, although some keepers opt to feed adult ball pythons every 10 -14 days. Do not rely on the advice of "only feeding your snake once a month," especially for young and growing snakes. This will leave you with a perpetually hungry (and thin) snake that is possibly more inclined to bite out of desperation for a meal.

Live vs. Pre-killed

Like other python species, with a little patience it is fairly easy to condition the ball python to accept and eat pre-killed or frozen/thawed prey items. The primary benefit to feeding pre-killed prey is avoiding injury to your ball python. Contrary to popular rumors as those often bandied about in Internet chat forums, ball pythons do not "need the hunt" or "need the kill" associated with feeding live rodents. Ball pythons will strike and constrict pre-killed prey when conditioned to do so, often as fervently as they would a live rodent.

Live rodents can seriously injure and/or kill a ball python if they are left unsupervised. Occasionally rodents are extremely aggressive. In this case, do not expect your ball python to "naturally defend itself" against

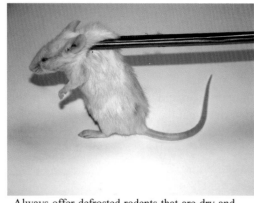

Always offer defrosted rodents that are dry and warm.

an attacking mouse or rat, as most often it won't. This is a very unnatural act; rodents will avoid snakes at all cost until they are housed together. Snakes are not programmed to deal with a rodent gnawing on them as a food or moisture source. Domestic rodents may lose some of their natural fear of reptiles and may be more inclined to test the limits of predator and prey. Many keepers have been surprised to find a mortally wounded or dead snake after leaving a mouse or rat in with it overnight (or even an hour). Mice can be especially bad about chewing on snakes, particularly when hungry, and can easily gnaw through a ball python's skin in a short period of time, causing injuries that may require the snake to be euthanized.

Training a snake to eat pre-killed prey isn't difficult and usually requires just a little patience and ingenuity on the keeper's part

A suitably sized bulge for an appropriate meal.

32

(which will be covered in the next section).

Frozen rodents should always be thoroughly thawed and warmed prior to feeding. Leaving the rodent near your snake's cage to thaw overnight may help entice a feeding response as the snake smells the warming prey. Hot water can also be used to thaw rodents, but it is suggested that the rodents be placed into a plastic bag first, to avoid them becoming too soggy. NEVER defrost rodents using a microwave oven – this can turn into a less-than-appetizing experience involving a meat grenade and its aftermath . . . a disgusting mess. A good trick to know when offering frozen defrosted rodents is using soiled rodent bedding taken from a cage of breeder rodents to excite a ball python. The warmed rodent can be rubbed down with the bedding to give it the live animal smell which may entice a reluctant feeder. Another trick is to put some of the bedding into the snake's cage prior to offering the defrosted rodent and to wait a bit for the animal to become excited before offering the food item.

Tricks to feeding defrosted rodents: Sometimes we can encourage a snake to take a defrosted, dry and warmed rodent after it has been rolled around in soiled mouse bedding. This added scent may be what is needed to encourage a reluctant snake to accept this form of prey item. I have also taken used mouse or rat bedding and placed it in a snakes cage fifteen minutes prior to offering a defrosted rodent to excite the snake into thinking it is about to be fed a live prey item. As a last resort gerbil bedding can be used in the same fashion to excite reluctant feeders. Keeping a few "pet" rodents has benefits and helps you appreciate the reality of feeding live prey.

I have had many pet rats that amazed me with their intelligence and gentle nature; I was very sad to witness their short 2 – 2.5 year lifespans. I do not enjoy feeding live prey since I am an animal lover by nature and I do not appreciate cruelty towards rodents. If you have to euthanize a prey animal, do it quickly and cleanly. Have a conscience and appreciate the animal's feelings.

From time to time, the ball python keeper may experience an extremely picky snake that will only take live prey. All efforts to convert the snake to pre-killed prey should be exhausted before resorting to feeding live, and it is the keeper's responsibility to supervise both snake and rodent any time live prey is offered.

Methods of Offering Prey

One of the easiest methods for feeding pre-killed prey is to condition your ball python to accept rodents offered on feeding tongs. Tongs, hemostats, and forceps are easily obtained through any major reptile supply company. To offer your ball python a rodent using tongs, grasp the prey item on the back, just above the front legs; doing so will give you more control over the prey item and also will make it easier for the snake to grab. Dangling a rodent by the tail makes it a hard target for the ball python to hit. If your snake is hungry, it will typically key right in on the rodent and strike. Occasionally you may need to wiggle the rodent to get the snake's attention. When the snake grabs the rodent, release it from the tongs. Once the snake has struck at and constricted the rodent, you

can give the tail of the prey item a gentle tug or two. This extra movement will often cause the python to constrict harder, thus reducing the chance of the snake losing interest in and dropping the prey item.

For snakes already conditioned to eat pre-killed prey, one can simply introduce the prey item into the snake's enclosure, leaving it in a place where the snake will encounter and subsequently consume it. Many keepers rely upon this method to feed their ball pythons.

Keep in mind: Don't "slap feed" or smack your ball python about the face when offering a rodent off tongs. Ball pythons are shy feeders and actions like this can turn off the snake's feeding response.

Always bleach or otherwise disinfect your feeding tongs between snakes if feeding multiple animals to avoid cross-contamination.

Tricks for Picky Feeders

One of the biggest complaints ball python keepers voice when initially making the switch to pre-killed prey is that the snake seems interested but just won't grab the rodent, or it strikes at the keeper instead of the rodent. Often this is due to the ball python "keying in" on the keeper's heat signature instead of the rodent's. The ball python's upper lip is lined with heat-sensing pits that allow it to focus in on

Three animals that are the same age, only one has eaten a few times (right animal).

warm-blooded prey in complete darkness. A room-temperature rodent may not offer enough heat for the ball python to follow. Using a heating pad to thoroughly heat the entire rodent for 10-15 minutes prior to feeding usually helps. Another method

A skinny snake in need of immediate attention.

is to hold the rodent's head up to a light bulb for 30 seconds or so before offering it to the snake. The point here is to create enough heat to catch your ball python's attention and elicit a feeding strike. A keeper may sometimes test the limits of how long a food item sits on a heat source. We are not trying to cook the rodent. The smell of this is unmistakable.

If your ball python seems finicky when initially making the switch to pre-killed prey, skip feeding the snake for a week or two. Sometimes ball pythons are shy feeders and prefer to eat after the lights have gone out at night. Offering prey at this time may induce an otherwise picky feeder to eat. Also try leaving a thawed rodent in the enclosure overnight for the snake to consume as it wishes. Disturb a shy feeder as little as possible after offering prey.

On occasion, adding another hide box or crumpling up newspaper for the ball python to hide under may help a shy feeder feel more secure and elicit a feeding response.

Ball pythons often will not feed while going through a shed cycle.

Allow your snake to digest for at least a day before handling again.

Where to Feed

There is a long-standing debate among reptile keepers over the best place to feed one's snake. Some advise that a snake should always be fed in a separate container than its cage so that the animal doesn't always assume it will be fed when a keeper opens the enclosure. One could as strongly argue that feeding a python in a separate cage or "feeding box" will condition the snake to expect food every time it is removed from its enclosure.

Snakes are instinctual creatures that can be conditioned to behave in a certain manner at particular times. Feeding is a great example of this. Pythons often display what is called a "feeding response," in which they may meet anything warm coming into the enclosure with a feeding strike, based on their nature as opportunistic feeders. This behavior, however, is very easy to read and anticipate, especially as you get to know your ball python's demeanor and normal habits. Since ball pythons are shy snakes by nature, it is neither necessary nor recommended to remove them from their enclosures for feeding. Suddenly placing the snake in a new, unfamiliar environment is often enough to disturb the animal into not feeding, causing the animal undue stress on top of missing a meal. Developing a routine with your ball python will allow the snake to anticipate being fed, especially if this is done at the same day and time each week. Additionally, it will give you as a keeper the opportunity to learn what behaviors constitute a feeding response for your ball python and use this to your advantage while offering prey. If you notice your snake locating itself in its hide with the head at the front, this snake is waiting to ambush a rodent. You may notice your snake suddenly responding to you entering the room. You have conditioned the snake to realize your presence may mean food.

An established snake can often be conditioned to follow or anticipate certain routines.

Assist-feeding and Force-feeding

These techniques are often used when a snake fails to feed and resulting weight loss threatens the animal's life. We sometime encounter hatchling snakes that refuse to eat anything offered

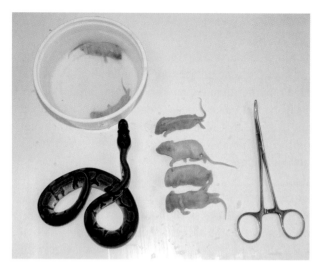

regardless how perfect their environment may appear. These animals don't seem to understand what food is and may require assist-feeding or force-feeding to activate a feeding response and also to "kick start" the snake's metabolism. After the initial post-hatch shed, most baby ball pythons should eat within a four to five week period. If the snake continues to refuse food and appears to be losing weight, it may be time to intervene.

Force-feeding is a last resort measure; ensure that you have exhausted all options for enticing the snake to feed (i.e. changing prey items and environmental conditions) prior to doing so, as this process tends to be stressful on the snake. **Additionally, it is strongly recommended that you seek guidance from a fellow snake keeper who is experienced at force-feeding, prior to trying it on your own.**

This process requires a small frozen fuzzy mouse defrosted in water, small forceps or hemostats, and a steady pair of hands. Having an assistant to hold the snake may also make the process easier. First attempts are known as assist feeding. Assist feeding allows the natural response of the animal to begin feeding once food is place in its mouth. Make sure the feeder rodent is small; this will make the job much easier and lessens the potential for damage to the snake. Hold the rodent's head at ear-level between the forceps. Gently use the nose of the mouse to prod the snake into opening its mouth. Once the mouth is open place the rodent's head down the snake's throat so the head is starting to disappear down the gullet. Water should be used as a lubricant. If the fuzzy mouse is not wet with water this process may be difficult. Gently place the snake down, holding its mouth over the rodent and release your grip and remain still. Some snakes may wait a minute or two and then begin to work the rodent down. If this happens do not move as this

Gently hold the snake behind the head.

may startle the snake and your effort may be lost. If a snake detects movement while eating it may stop feeding, a snake is vulnerable while eating its prey. Many babies will frantically try to spit out the rodent. As they do this they coat the feed animal with saliva, making the next attempt easier. If the rodent is spit back out try again to push the rodent further down and repeat the process.

If a snake-versus-keeper battle occurs a stronger approach, known as force feeding, may be required. If the snake continues to spit out the rodent, push the rodent all the way down the throat and gently massage the rodent down a few inches and then put the snake down. Some snakes may attempt to spit up the rodent. If this occurs, tickle the snake's tail and encourage it to crawl forward until it begins to flick its tongue. This single point can be very helpful when dealing with stubborn snakes and can make the snake think about some-thing else other than spitting up its meal. Bigger

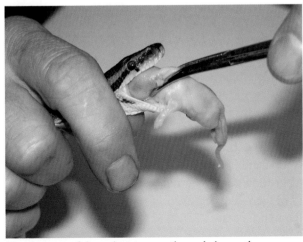

Use the nose of the rodent to open the snake's mouth.

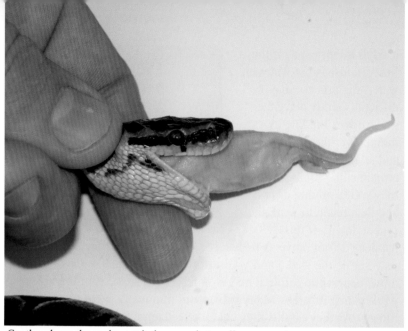

Gently release the snake, set it down, and stop all movement.

snakes can be fed in the exact same manner with larger-sized food animals. Always soak the defrosted rodent in water and attempt feeding with a soaking wet rodent; a dry feeder animal can rip or damage the delicate tissue of a snake's esophagus.

Assist feeding may be done weekly until the snake expresses interest in feeding on its own. This technique helps stimulate the animal's metabolism as the food item is digested. Between assist feeding and force feeding sessions, offer food items as usual until the snake begins to feed on its own.

Many snakes may begin to swallow after this procedure is attempted a few times.

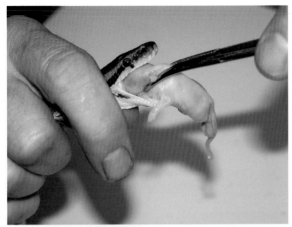

A resistent assist feeder needs a bit stronger action.

Gently press a thumb along the ventral area to pass the rodent down to the stomach area.

Once the snake flicks its tongue and begins to crawl,
the procedure is complete.

Shedding

Ball pythons will periodically shed their skin throughout the course of
their lives. Shedding may correlate with growth or events such as
breeding, egg-laying, and even disease or injury. Paying attention to
shed cycles and noting what is normal for your ball python(s) during
this event can be a useful herp keeping tool.

As a snake grows, the outermost layer of skin will gradually wear
out and will need to be replaced with a new layer. The faster a
snake grows (i.e. the more it eats), the sooner this process will
occur.

On average a baby snake may shed every month or two, and a
larger adult snake may shed with less frequency. Ill or injured
snakes may shed frequently as the body heals.

The process of shedding (called *Ecdysis*) usually takes 10-14 days
from start to finish. To further understand this, let's break it down
into stages.

Stage 1: The snake takes on a general dull appearance and ventral scales may take on a pinkish coloration. The change in ventral (belly) scales is often the earliest indicator of an impending shed and also frequently causes alarm among inexperienced keepers. Ball pythons may also refuse food at this time.

Snake sheds stretch and are larger than the snakes that made them.

Stage 2: "Going opaque/blue." This is the part of the shedding process with which most are familiar. The snake's eyes turn a milky, opaque blue-gray and the entire body takes on a hazy, faded appearance. This is caused by a film of fluid building up between the outer layer of skin and the new skin underneath. The skin is fragile during this period, making the snake more vulnerable to injury, and most ball pythons will not feed while "opaque" or "in blue". It is highly recommended that one not offer live prey at this point. The fluid layer also reduces a ball python's eyesight at this time, often making the snake extremely shy or even cranky; a normally docile, quiet ball may be more likely to nip a keeper out of defensiveness while in this stage of the shed cycle.

Stage 3: Preparation for shedding. At this point, the new layer of skin has developed. The body will remain dull in appearance, but the ball python's eyes will clear up and no longer look opaque. This may last for 4 – 6 days prior to actually sloughing off the old skin.

Stage 4: Sloughing. At this point, the snake typically rubs its face on any and all cage fixtures, loosening the outer layer of old skin from around the nose and head. It will continue to rub the old skin back as it crawls forward, turning the skin inside out as it goes. If the snake has a full shed, the sloughed skin may end up in a wadded, crinkled

A snake going opaque.

"doughnut," or be stretched across the cage in one long piece. Afterwards, the freshly shed ball python has a crisp, clean appearance. This is usually a perfect time to take photos!

Husbandry Tip: Humidity

Your ball python's success in shedding is a good indicator of humidity within the enclosure, as well as the snake's overall health. A thriving, robust ball python with proper humidity levels will typically shed in one solid piece, leaving the old skin like a rolled up sock. A snake that is exposed to dry conditions or left without a consistent source of fresh, clean water may retain parts of its shed skin, rubbing the rest off in scattered flakes throughout the enclosure.

A large water dish allows a snake to seek out moisture and to soak.

Chapter 4. Selecting a Healthy Ball Python

While ball pythons can make excellent "pet" snakes and are widely available, it is important to be well-informed prior to acquisition to ensure you choose the right animal.

First off make sure you are prepared to keep a pet python - expectations of what it is. Will you feed live food if needed? A pet python could live to the ripe old age of 40 but ages over 20 years should be expected. The reason for keeping a ball python over some of the larger growing boids is size and tractability. Have you kept any other snakes? As previously discussed, snakes have a specialized set of care requirements that must be met in order for the animal to thrive.

What do all those letters mean?

If you've done some research (and hopefully you have by this point), you've probably noticed ball pythons labeled as WC, CH, CBB, CB,

USCB, "imported" or "farmed." So just what do all those letters and terms mean, and how do they affect you as the potential ball python keeper?

CBB – "Captive Bred and Born." This means that the hatchling ball python hatched from eggs that were laid in captivity by parents that were already in captivity and subsequently bred, hence producing those eggs. Sometimes "USCB" is used here, to denote animals that were bred and hatched in the United States.

CB – This is a term that can go two ways. Some folks use it to denote Captive Born offspring, which can include animals from eggs that came from wild-collected females but were hatched in captivity. It can also mean Captive Bred, from parents already in captivity. Bottom line here is to ask the seller what they mean by "CB". An honest seller should be willing and able to give you thorough background information on their snakes.

CH – "Captive-Hatched." This specifically means babies hatched from eggs taken from gravid, wild-collected females. The eggs are laid in captivity and then hatched, and the females released, or used for skins or food. A great number of captive-hatched ball pythons are imported into the U.S. every year, and the majority of these find their way into retail pet stores.

"Farmed / Farm-Raised" – Generally this is exactly the same as captive-hatched. Gravid females are collected and held while they lay and incubate eggs. Sometimes eggs are taken from the females and artificially incubated, while other times the females are left to incubate the eggs themselves. When the babies hatch, they are typically shipped overseas and the females are either released or skinned.

"Imported" – This can describe either captive-hatched or wild-caught animals. Either way, the animal originated from somewhere outside of the United States.

"WC" – Wild-Caught. Animals are collected out of their natural environment and exported to the United States (or other countries). Wild-caught animals often carry parasites, both internal and external, can be extremely difficult to acclimate to a captive lifestyle, and are best left to experienced keepers.

Reptile Specialty Stores and Pet Stores

A reliable local supplier of reptiles – if there is one in your area – can be a valuable resource for obtaining healthy animals as well as husbandry equipment, supplies, and information. Visiting a specialty store gives you the opportunity to see animals in person prior to making a purchase, as well as allowing you to observe the conditions in which reptiles are kept at that location. A store with competent, experienced staff will also be able to lend husbandry advice, recommend favorite products, and put you in touch with other reptile keepers, allowing you to develop a broader perspective on reptile care. Finding a person that really "knows" their animals can be a great bonus when it comes to trouble-shooting problems and helping with husbandry issues. Keep in mind that while a pet store may carry or even specialize in reptiles, it doesn't always guarantee the quality of animals, staff experience, or advice you may receive. Check with local herpetological societies and even research the Internet for locations in or near your area with a good, established reputation for providing quality animals, supplies, and advice.

Snake Selection Criteria

Overall Appearance and Behavior

Does the snake appear to be healthy, robust, and alert? Look for a snake with good body weight and muscle tone. A healthy ball python should not be listless, limp, or weak. Optimally, the snake should sit calmly, or move about slowly with long, even tongue flicks, although a young snake rolled into a defensive ball shouldn't be penalized for doing what comes naturally. A nervous snake that flails about and tries to escape should be avoided.

Body

When held, the snake should feel solid and stout, not squishy, bloated, thin, or bony. Pay attention to the snake as it moves through your hands. Feel along the ribs for lumps that could indicate broken bones.

If a snake does not appear healthy, then it is probably not.

Skin

A healthy ball python's skin should be smooth and free of any sores, blisters, wounds, or external parasites such as ticks or mites. If ticks are present, they will be imbedded in the skin. Mites appear as little "poppyseeds" walking on the snake or clustered around the eyes. Check your hands for black specks after holding the snake, as this would indicate the presence of snake mites as well.

Eyes

The eyes of a healthy ball python should be clear, with no sign of puffiness, cloudiness (except for an impending shed), pus, infection, or parasites. Blue or grey eyes are not an indication of illness, but simply an indicator of an impending shed. Tiny black "poppy seeds" surrounding the spectacle are mites (ectoparasites) and snakes with mites should be avoided. Animals with retained spectacles from previous sheds should also be avoided. Wrinkled eyecaps may be a sign of low humidity or a poor shed and are not an indicator of poor health.

48

Mouth

The mouth should be closed as the ball python moves about. Excessive yawning or opening of the mouth can indicate a respiratory infection, as does a great

A healthy mouth is light pink, clean, and contains minimal fluid.

amount of saliva or bubbling in the mouth. The gums and mouth tissue should be a healthy light whitish-pink color, without reddened areas or broken teeth. If you are not comfortable opening the snake's mouth, ask the seller to do so for you. A puffy, distended throat is caused by the animal exhaling through its glottis (breathing tube / trachea located inside the mouth) and is an indicator of an upper respiratory infection. In these cases, the snake is failing to push the air out through its nostrils since they are clogged with mucous.

Vent

The animal's vent should be clean and not crusted with stuck feces. It should not be swollen, red, or puffy, and there should be no retained shed and no discharge.

A normal vent.

Consider the age of the animal you intend to purchase. While many potential owners like the idea of raising a snake from a hatchling, sometimes brand new snakes and brand new snake keepers aren't always the best combination. Extremely young ball pythons are less forgiving of husbandry errors than an older animal will be. New keepers make mistakes as part of the learning process, and it is something that every reptile keeper will

A crusty vent indicates a period of heavy breeding or a possible bacterial or protozoan infection.

experience. An older snake (6 months - 1 year) that is well-started and accustomed to people will be better prepared to weather the occasional "newbie mistake" than a tiny, delicate hatchling.

When choosing younger animals, try to find babies that have eaten at least 5-6 meals on an established feeding regime.

Special Note: Transporting your Snake

Preparing a transportation container for your new ball python will lessen the stress of a changing environment. Styrofoam coolers or commercial fish boxes make excellent containers in which to transport a ball python as they prevent exposure to rapid changes in temperature.

The proper transportation setup - An insulated styrofoam box with a few holes, heat pads (for when it is cold), and the snake placed in a pillow case with crumpled newspaper.

Chapter 5: Common Health Concerns

Note the ticks in the skin fold under the chin of this ball python.

Ticks and Mites

These are ectoparasites that feed on blood from their hosts. Mites and ticks are factors of stress. They are generally easy to remove but should be carefully approached if you are new to this problem. Mites are the size of a poppy seed and are typically black. They move slowly about on the animal and are easily squished between fingers, leaving a smudge of blood. In worse case situations the snake may appear thin and dehydrated as heavy loads of mites can make an animal anemic and threaten its overall health.

Ticks are larger, closer to the size of a split pea. They are indicators of wild-collected animals and easy enough to mechanically remove or kill with commercial tick treatments. It is always better to purchase an animal that is free of these parasites. Rely on the seller to solve the problem prior to your purchase. This ensures you will not take the problem home and further irritate the snake. Visual inspection of the animal is the best way to determine the cause of this problem. Raised scales may be indicators of a tick lodged and feeding below the scale. Watch the animal closely and inspect for any movement or activity of mites crawling on the snake.

Look under the snake in the crease that runs from the front tip of the jaw to the throat. Mites will often locate themselves in this area and are easy to see against the white skin background. Animals with swollen, puffy, or abnormal eyes should be studied. Mites will lodge themselves around the spectacle of the eye and may cause irritation, swelling, and retained eye caps. Pass the animal through your hands and note if any living black dots are left behind. This is a simple and quick check that will often reveal the presence of mites.

Ticks

Larger than a mite, this ectoparasite appears most commonly on wild-caught animals. Removal is done manually with a pair of tweezers or forceps. Grab the tick and spin it clockwise. This will force the tick to lose its grip and break free from the snake's skin. If left on the animal it will continue to suck blood or it may release itself from the snake and become free-roaming, looking for a new host. Once they are removed, drop them into a cup of alcohol or water and bleach solution, or flush them down the toilet.

Mites

Mites suck, quite literally. This small, bloodthirsty parasite is the bane of just about any herper as mites are very prolific and challeng-ing to

Using forceps to remove a tick.

eradicate once their presence is
established.

The snake mite is a minute
ectoparasite very similar in
appearance to a tear-shaped
poppy seed. A mite infestation is
about as much fun for the snake
as a raging case of head lice is
for a human. Severe mite cases
can result in an anemic, dehydrated animal, to the point of
becoming life-threatening. Mites
also carry disease and pathogens
from one host to the other and

Mites will appear in a snake's water
dish. (These are poppy seeds. No
actual mites were injured during the
production of this photograph.)

are a wonderful way to infect all other cage mates, as well as other
snakes housed in the area of the primary infestation.

Mites are often found in the bottom of the snake's water dish or
crawling on the rim of it. Examine the snake closely, with special
attention to the underside of the snake's jaw. Look for black specks
between the white scales. Swollen or puffy eyes should also be
examined for a mite infestation surrounding the spectacle. Mites will
often locate in numbers around the eyes if the infestation goes
unnoticed. The saliva of the mite irritates the tissue and will cause
damage to the delicate area of the eye and will often result in retained eyecaps.

How to Fight A Mite

The quickest way to remove a heavy load of mites is to soak the
infested snake in a cage-temperature bath.

Snake mites are incapable of swimming, and leaving a snake to soak
overnight in shallow water will drown many of these arachnid pests.
Adding a small amount of dish soap to the water will help to coat the
mites and speed the drowning process. The depth of the water
should only be deep enough to cover half of the animal's body. The
water will drown many of the mites and ensure the animal has a
chance to re-hydrate.

Pouring water over the snake will also aid in drowning any of the little bastards that think they can ride out the storm on the snake's back. A thorough cleaning of the cage with a hot solution of mild detergent and bleach is a must with moderate to heavy infestations. This

Soaking a snake in tepid water will help reduce a mite infestation, but will not kill all of the mites.

will reduce the number of adult mites and their eggs. The mite begins its days sucking blood from the snake. As it grows it will leave the safety of living under the snake's scales looking for a safe area to lay its eggs. They will often climb to the highest corners of the cage to lay its eggs. This is one of the areas to focus on when cleaning the enclosure. Hot water kills mites and their eggs. Mites are very good at what they do and can lay dormant for what seems ages before they reinfest the animal's enclosure, much to the keeper's surprise.

When treating your snake and its cage always pay special attention to

Commercial mite and tick remedies. Follow the directions carefully!

cleaning all cage furniture. Remember that moving the animal from one location to another can spread mites! What is the magical remedy? Ask your local reptile dealer what they use. Everyone has their own favorite remedy. Products that are commercially available such as Provent-A-Mite® and Reptile Relief® are effective. Pay special attention to the directions. Failure to follow them can harm your animal. These products poison the mites and if not used correctly can hurt the snake. Never treat a dehydrated snake with a mite product. Always offer water first. This is critical! Do not use mite remedies containing pesticides (permethrin, etc.) around any pet invertebrates like tarantulas or scorpions – move them out of the room you intend to treat unless you want dead pet inverts.

Stuck Sheds

Often sick or weak snakes will show their immediate problems when in this condition. If the animal appears trapped in its own skin like a mummy and looks uncomfortable while other snakes look healthy, this may be an animal to avoid. You may inquire about the animal and wish to see it after the problem has been fixed a few days later. I have seen snakes that were miserably trapped within their own sheds shed out and look flawless! A dried out "crusty" ball python does not often appeal to an educated buyer.

Retained Eye Caps

Retained eye caps will appear as a rippled creased, or cracked spectacle covering both or one of the animal's eyes. We often note a white edge around the eye where the last shed occurred, leaving the eye cap on. This generally occurs when the animal has been kept

Patches of stuck shed and retained eye caps are evident on this ball python.

overly dry and may have not had appropriate humidity or water contact needed to complete its last shed. In worse case scenarios we have seen snakes with multiple eye caps, which must certainly must be uncomfortable for the animal. Generally this is an easy fix, and a soak in a locking plastic storage container with air holes in tepid 85° F water for a 24-hour period will help soften the skin for removal.

When soaking the snake, make sure that it is left in a container where the water depth passes no further than halfway up the snake's side. Deeper water may cause a python to panic and increase the possibility of drowning.

After a long soak, a safe way to remove a retained eye cap is to use a wet Q-tip to lift the edge of the stuck shed. With the edge of your finger-nail try to lift the edge of the eye cap and peel it off.

Upper Respiratory Infections and Pneumonia

When observing a ball python for purchase, note that frequent yawning, gaping, gasping, or opening of the mouth is often an

A foamy and wet mouth are signs of a possible upper respiratory infection.

indicator of an upper respiratory infection and is something to avoid. Better to point out the condition to the seller and allow them to correct the problem.

One of the biggest problems we observe in captive ball pythons is respiratory distress caused by the combination of low ambient humidity, improper ambient temperatures, and a screen-top enclosure, which basically allows the environment within the snake's cage to be affected by any external influences in the room in which the snake is kept. Keep in mind that if you have a screen top on the enclosure you will probably want to cover it most or all of the way with plastic or a towel to keep moisture from escaping. Proper, reliable ambient temperatures (back to that thermometer!) are important as warm air holds more moisture than cool air. You want the enclosure to be humid, not WET. A soggy cage can eventually lead to serious bacterial and fungal infections and consequently, death. Symptoms of an upper respiratory may include: Wet mouth, frothing, and/or crust around the animal's lips, blowing bubbles, bloody mucous, substrate sticking to the animal's face, gurgling, whistling sounds, hacking, and inflation of the chin area.

Unlike humans, snakes have a single primary lung. When relaxed, a snake's lung is filled with air. Muscle contractions expel air and allow for a new breath. This respiration process is the opposite of humans. We have to expand our lungs to take a new breath.

The keeper may sometimes note the snake arching its back. This is the animal trying to deal with fluids building up in the single usable lung. Snakes do not have the ability to cough like we do. They will often suffocate as they try to deal with mucous in the lung as their pulmonary system is primitive and inefficient at ridding itself of such things. When arching its back, the snake is trying to drain the fluids to the rear or front of the lung or where the animal may attempt to expel the phlegm. In severe cases, the fluid appears whitish-yellow with a pudding-like consistency. This is often an indication of pneumonia. The risk lies when a snake attempts to expel mucous from the lung; frequently this mucous creates a blockage in the trachea and the snake suffocates from lack of oxygen. In some cases, blood vessels in the lung dilate to full capacity as the animal struggles to take oxygen from the lung into the bloodstream. If the animal's lung has a great deal of fluid within this area it is inefficient, since all of the blood vessels can't come into contact with oxygen-laden air. The need for oxygen may be so great that blood vessels burst and the resulting hemorrhage releases blood into the lung, creating problems such as suffocation, blood loss, and further infection. Blood is a perfect medium for bacteria and can account for a new life-threatening infection.

Treatment – Correct the possible points of stress with special attention to heat and cleanliness. If the conditions are not proper for a healthy animal it will never have a chance to fight off the infection. Disinfect the water bowl on a daily basis to avoid recontamination. In mild cases, turning the heat up to optimal temperatures and some babying are all it takes to reverse the problem. If the conditions are severe the best course of action is a trip to an experienced reptile veterinarian. The veterinarian can culture the invading bacterium and choose the appropriate antibiotic therapy.

Common and Successful Prescription Antibiotics

Amikacin (Brand name Amaglyde-V®) – Injectable broad-spectrum antibiotic that is very effective on many gram-negative bacteria that often infect cold blooded animals. First dose @ 5mg/kg of well hydrated body weight. Next 7 doses are 2.5 mg/kg, half of the initial dose. Repeat these doses every 72 hours for another 7 treatments. Improvements may be noted within the first week. Very effective against respiratory infections, lesions, stomatitis and wounds. Negatives – if a ball python is dehydrated or in poor condition this drug may cause kidney damage. If possible, the animal must be properly hydrated for 24 hours before treatment.

Enrofloxin - (Brand name Baytril®) — Form - Injectable or oral. An effective, safe antibiotic that is often used in place of Amakacin when there is fear of possible kidney damage. Treatment injectable or oral @ 15 mg/kg daily for 10 – 14 days. Baytril injection is best diluted (ringers solution) from its original injectable state since it typically causes tissue sloughing at the injection site.

Ceftazidime (Brand name Fortaz®) - third generation cephalosporin. A newer injectable antibiotic that has a wide range effect on many bacteria. Works well on respiratory infections and aggressive deep seated infections. Injections are 20 –30 mg/kg every 72 hours for 7 – 10 treatments. Starts as a powder that is constituted in saline or ringers and then frozen. Once constituted into solution it must remain frozen until used. It remains stable for only 24 hours after reconstituted at room temperature and 7 days if refrigerated.

Injections - Injected in the first third (front) intra muscular in meaty tissue adjacent to the spine. Note, do not inject near the spine or in the lower 2/3 of the animal's body near the kidneys. This is best performed by a veterinarian or a person with experience concerning the correct methods of animal injections.

Scale Rot / Belly Rot

Scale or Belly Rot is a condition due to thermal burns and/or unsanitary cage conditions. A heating pad that creates an intense hot spot with cold cage air temps will cause the animal to cling to this dangerous heat source. The snake's need for heat over rides its limited ability to discern if the cage floor temperature is safe. The result is a thermal burn that destroys the tissue in contact. First signs are pinkish belly scales; do not mistake this with the occasional pinkish hue the keeper may notice when the snake is in the middle of a shed. Serious conditions are when the belly area has actually rotted through into the body cavity opening the animal up for massive infection. A slight case will need ointment treatment such as a topical triple antibiotic cream applied twice daily for 7-10 days religiously. The best treatment is a prescribed Silvedene ointment from a Veterinarian. Once the tissue is severely damaged and rots, the wound has to be cleaned and systemic antibiotic therapy needs to take place. A veterinarian is needed in this case, without hard-hitting antibiotics the infection will often destroy the animal. Make sure the cage has correct temperatures; avoid cheap small heating pads that fail to provide a proper heat source. Never depend on a hot rock as a sufficient heat source, this does not provide a large enough surface area to heat the animal to its desired range. Filthy cage conditions and wetness can allow aggressive bacterial infections to damage tissue that is in contact with dirty bedding and moisture. Keep the cage clean, warm and dry and this will not happen.

Treatment – Correct the problem. Remove substrate and replace with white paper towels. Topical antibiotic creams twice daily. Frequent shallow warm water soaks, finish by rinsing wounds with diluted two parts water one part betadine.

Infective Stomatitis AKA "Mouth Rot"

A healthy ball python's mouth should seat together and not expose areas of tissue or teeth. If you see unusual areas where the mouth does not shut well or unhealthy exposed tissue this may be signs of infective stomatitis AKA "mouth rot". This condition is a syndrome of mechanical trauma to the animals mouth and gums due possibly to incorrect caging, cage furniture or the environment that the snake is being kept in. "Mouth rot" is not a disease just as a hang nail is not! Opportunistic bacteria causing an infection can cause cankers and areas of necrotic tissue. This also should be avoided and pointed out to the seller. Healthy gums are a light pink white without marks or veining. Small red spots and lesions are an indication of petechia that are some of the first symptoms of stress leading to mouth rot. In a more advanced stage mouth rot appears as cankers and cheese like material caking the animals mouth. As it advances healthy tissue and teeth are lost to the infection and if left untreated a systemic infection spreading throughout the animal's body is a very real threat to the animal's life.

Treatment – Correct points of stress with special attention to damaging fixtures within the snakes immediate environment, heat and cleanliness. Cleaning the wound – In the early stages with minimal to moderate tissue damage applying antibiotic cream or rinsing with diluted two parts water to one part betadine the mouth and gums twice daily. If there is dead tissue build up it is best to rinse this away with warm water if possible. The animal will have to be held under a faucet and positioned so that the stream of water washes this necrotic dead tissue and mucous away. As the condition advances in severity it is best to debride the mouth of all unhealthy tissue, this involves removing the dead and dying infectious tissue. A dilute solution of two parts water, one part hydrogen peroxide oral rinse will help to loosen this tissue. This process can be painful for the animal and may be easier to perform by rinsing the snakes mouth out and leaving it in a shallow soak of warm water for several hours to a day. Locate a third of a plastic storage box for soaking on a heat pad and monitor the soak temperature, 85° to 95° F is optimal. This technique will help rid the animal of the necrotic tissue, hydrate it and elevate its body temperature. Many snakes can be left in this type of soak for days, clean water daily, note the amount of material from the snakes mouth in the water. The removal of dead tissue and antibiotic ointments and/or rinses allows the animal immune system to better deal with the infection. If large amounts of dead tissue are left unchecked it provides a haven for infection and the condition only worsens. Severe cases will attack bone and systemic anti biotic therapy is a must via injectable antibiotics.

Eye Infections

Eye infections present themselves as cloudy eyes, swollen eyes, or swelling of the lip under the eye. We sometimes see this type of condition and it is advisable to seek immediate veterinarian attention. The eye area is very difficult to treat since it is a perfect part of the body to encase an infection. Aggressive topical opthalmic tissue-penetrating antibiotics are often needed to battle the invading bacteria. If left untreated the snake's life will often be in danger.

Topical Ointments – Bacitracin, Polysporin, Neosporin – for use on shallow, superficial wounds. Treat twice daily. Povodone Iodine, such as Betadine solution, is excellent for use in irrigating wounds and debriding infected tissue. Hydrogen peroxide diluted with two parts water also works well for infected areas or wounds. This solution will help remove dead and dying tissue from the wound.

Rodent Bites

These wounds should be cleaned with diluted anti bacterial rinse such as betadine or provoiodine, pack twice daily with antibiotic ointment. If severe bites occur that require stiches seek aid of a veterinarian. Without proper treatment moderate wounds can become infected and the animal may

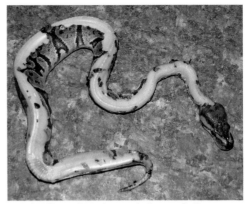

Leaving live rodents in a snake's cage for long periods can yield horrible results. A mouse attacked this snake.

turn septic and die. Treating the snake with a systemic antibiotic, topical ointment and proper wound treatment is critical if this occurs.

Dermal Fungal Infection

Dermal fungal infections develop if the snake is exposed to unsanitary, cool moist conditions for prolonged periods of time it may develop patches or lesions where the skin appears unhealthy. These patches may scab over or lose the shine of the scales, some areas may appear raised and ultimately be confused as a burn. Treatment

A ball python with healed belly rot. Note the crease-like scar.

is to correct the husbandry and keep the animal clean, dry and warm. Use betadine or povodone iodine solution topically on the areas twice daily for 10 days or until the animal shows definate improvement.

Internal Parasites

Internal parasites are typically diagnosed from an animal failing to thrive and are usually seen in wild-collected animals. Typically internal parasites are not a problem for most captive ball pythons but animals failing to thrive under proper conditions should be checked

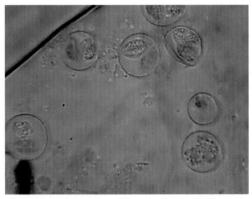

Coccidia and protozoa. Photo by Dean Wallace, DVM.

parasites. A veterinarian can play a major role in defining the exact problem. A stool sample, fresh within 24 hours kept in a refrigerator, in your best tupper ware or zip lock bag is all you need to bring to the veterinarian. If the stool sample is yellow and white, urates, this will not suffice. If you are unable to get this sample a cloacal wash can be performed to flush the lower GI system for the problem. This procedure is done at the clinic and will reveal the possible source of a problematic snake.

Parasite Overview - These are most of the parasitic infections to consider. If treated properly the animal will often bounce back to a happy and healthy python. There are no

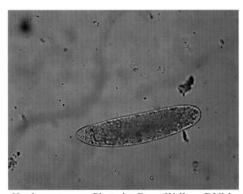

Hookworm ova. Photo by Dean Wallace DVM.

magical drops or cure-alls without first identifying the problem, many off-the-shelf remedies are weak and non-parasite specific. It is critical that the animal's weight is first known before any and all treatment. All parasite treatments are effective because they poison the host animal enough to kill the specific grouping of parasites but not enough to kill the snake. A veterinarian's advice is often critical regarding the correct approach and treatment, most applicable medications are prescription.

Picking a Reptile Veterinarian

In the event that your animal develops a problem and you need the assistance of a veterinarian, it is very important that you pick the right one. Read this book and understand the problem before you speak to the veterinarian. You will be better able to explain the situation and you may also determine if the veterinarian sounds knowledgable. If the chosen veterinarian does not inspire confidence, you may be wise to look further. Some "vets" may specialize in exotic animal medicine. These are your best choice. Use this book as a tool - It covers most issues that you will encounter with your ball python. You may find the text helpful to an open-minded veterinarian that wants to help but may not have experience with snake medical issues.

Chapter 6. Breeding & Egg Incubation

Sexing a Snake

This is either very easy to describe or very hard. Get someone who knows how to sex a snake properly and it is EASY! Tell someone that knows nothing about sexing a snake and it can be a bit of a challenge . . . to say the least.

While ball pythons are not sexually dimorphic in a strict sense, females generally grow larger than males, and males usually possess more pronounced cloacal spurs located on each side of the vent. A male ball python may also have a longer tail than a female of the same size. As each of these conditions can be quite variable, none provide a hard-and-fast rule for consistently and properly sexing ball pythons.

There are two established methods for determining the presence of heimpenes (male copulatory organs) in ball pythons, both of which are best done by a person versed in the technique.

Probing

Probing is a very reliable method of sexing a snake and involves inserting a polished, lubricated stainless steel probe into the snake's cloaca in the direction of the tail, passing into a hemipenis (if present). Sex is determined by measuring the depth to which the probe enters before meeting light resistance. Male ball pythons probe 5+ subcaudal scales, while females probe 2-3 subcaudal scales.

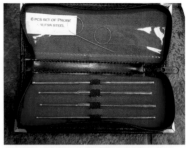

Commercially available set of probes.

Probing the Female

Use your finger tip to note the depth of the probe and then count the scale depth.

This female probes shallow - Three subcaudal scales.

Probing the Male

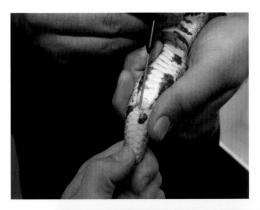

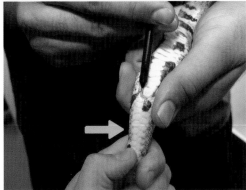

Probes go in deep on males.

Note the seven scale depth that was probed on this male.

Popping

The second technique is manually everting the males hemipenes, AKA "popping." This process involves a qualified keeper and looking for evidence of the male's reproductive equipment. Using two hands (a second person may be required to hold the snake), one thumb is used to pull the anal plate (scale covering the vent) slightly up and back, while the other thumb is used to push upward over the tail (starting low) towards the vent, in a motion that partially everts one or both hemipenes.

Popping the Male

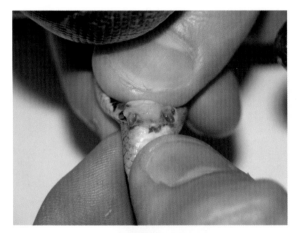

Hemipenes of a juvenile.

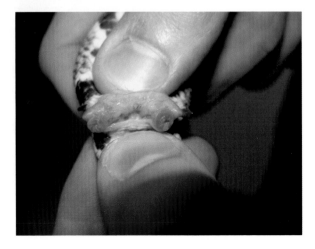

Hemipenes of an adult male.

Popping the Female

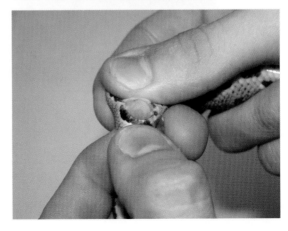

This method is most reliable on hatchling ball pythons; as they grow, male snakes develop muscle control over each hemipenis, making the snake difficult to pop. Larger animals can also be partially popped, looking for evidence of sperm plugs on a mature, reproductive male. Both techniques require care and can harm an animal if performed incorrectly. The best choice is to find someone that knows how to properly probe or pop a snake that is willing to give advice and instruction **before** you attempt either procedure. Obviously in this case your most invaluable resource is an experienced reptile breeder who has sexed hundreds – if not thousands – of snakes.

Also keep in mind that *some* veterinarians can sex an animal . . . not all, some. More than a few snakes turn up missexed every year by veterinary professionals who are simply inexperienced with either procedure, and how results may vary from species to species.

Breeding Age and Size

Male ball pythons typically reach sexual maturity within the first two years of age under a normal feeding schedule, while a female will often require three years or more to reach reproductive size. A sexually mature male is typically a 32 to 34" animal while a female

A 4-year old adult female ball python.

will need to be larger, in the 40" (1000 gram+) size range. The size of the female is critical as a female will have to be large enough to pass her eggs without becoming egg bound. Females have the potential to lay a clutch of eggs once per season in optimal conditions.

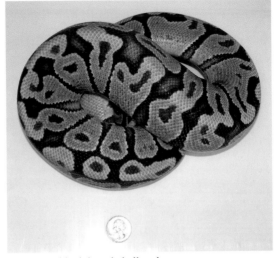

A 3-year old adult male ball python.

Many females may lay a clutch every other year under normal conditions.

Why breed ball pythons?

If you find yourself drawn to the world of snake keeping you may hope to attain the ultimate satisfaction, breeding and making your own snakes. Since ball pythons breed with relative ease it is feasible to breed ball pythons in any household. There is a certain pleasure felt when you open a container to see babies hatching out of their eggs. If you decide to invest in unusual morphs, you may actually enjoy being part of a hobby that has the potential to pay for itself (and more) while allowing you to roll money back into other mutations. There is always the potential to hatch out the next mutation that brings you a sense of accomplishment and notoriety from the ball python community. There are few hobbies that can actually pay for themselves while taking up minimal time and space.

Courting and Copulation

Male ball pythons will often rely on the use of their anal spurs to tickle and prod a prospective mate. These spurs are the remnants of ancestral legs and have no other use than for courtship. They are located on each side of the vent and are found on both sexes but are

71

Caught in the Act - A pair of ball pythons copulating.

typically more prominent on males. The male will generally align his body with the female's and begin to back down the female's body and tickle her into position until he can position his tail beneath the female's vent. The spurs will often cause the female to move which aids the male in positioning her. A non-reproductive female, a stubborn female, or another male may make copulation difficult without the aid of such spurs. Two males may engage in copulation out of desperation and confusion. This is purely for fun! Once the male is in the proper mating position he will evert a hemipene, one of two(hemi - denotes two), into the female's vent for introduction of the sperm. A pair may copulate for hours or even days. During this process the

The male ball python's spurs are used to tickle the female into position for mating.

female receives sperm from the male, which she retains for possible future fertilization.

It may take many copulations to yield a fertile clutch of eggs, or on occasion a single copulation may suffice. In captive breeding efforts I look for six solid copulations before pregnancy is achieved. Sperm is retained within the female and is released to mature ova during ovulation. A female may retain sperm for many months. This time period seems be reliant on a female's temperature and conditioning. If I were to set a safe length of time from last copulation to ovulation to produce fertile eggs I would try not to stretch it farther than a 25-day period. Over time sperm retention may lower viable sperm counts. Periods of high heat due to constant basking, summer temperatures, and such will often shorten the sperm's life within a female.

A wild snake will go through definite seasons with hot periods, which will "sterilize" any retained sperm if she did not become pregnant the previous season. This may be nature's way of providing a new sire the following year and offering the best viable sperm available for fertilization.

Breeding

Once sexually mature, ball pythons will often rely on change of seasons and artificial and natural triggers to exhibit reproductive activities. Ball python males will often court females at any time of the year but most females are not reproductive until the cooler months. As mentioned, a courting male will rely on its anal spurs to "tickle' the female to move into position and allow copulation. A non-receptive female will often hide from the male and not lift her tail when the male attempts to court her.

Captive breeding often coincides with our winter cycles here in North America. We often see breeding during fall, winter, and spring with lower activity during the warmer months. This is only made as a generalization and ball pythons have been bred during all months of the year. We often attempt to breed the snakes for 3-5 months before actual pregnancies or egg production. Breeding season begins with the onset of cooler nighttime temperatures where the temperature is gradually lowered to the mid to low 70s F over a 2-4 week period. It

73

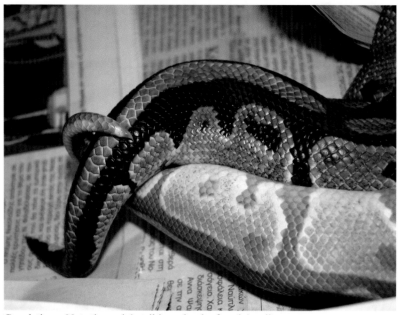
Copulation.   Note the male's tail is under the female's tail.

is critical to watch the health of the animals during this time as upper respiratory infections may occur if temperatures have become too low or the animal becomes stressed. The daytime temperature returns to a reasonable ambient temperature that allows basking and digestion of small meals. We will often provide ambient temps of 80 to 85° F with an essential basking period during the day. At night the temperature is determined by the room temperatures and no hot spot is provided within the enclosures. Be careful as stressed snakes may become sick if a basking spot is not provided. Often a few weeks of this type of temperature cycle will trigger an adult male to be interested in breeding. This temperature cycle may last 2-4 months to be effective. To further exaggerate this cycle we will often reduce the light cycle of the animal to 8-10 hours of daylight with greater periods of darkness. (During warmer months and when breeding is not the intent, we use a 12-14 hour day light cycle.) The reduction of light cycle and reduced temperatures act as triggers to encourage breeding activity. Some breeders may also incorporate light misting of the vivarium to boost humidity and create activity that may prove effective.

The theory of this cycle is the during this time the males' testosterone levels begin to elevate, which induces breeding. Also sperm production increases during this time. These environmental factors cause the male to seek out and to copulate with adult females. During this time, an over zealous male may attempt to breed other males and immature females.

During this cool period some breeders elect to stop all feeding while others may continue to feed their animals but reduce meal sizes to smaller prey items. With cooler temperatures food digestion is a bit harder on the animals and a large meal may prove too much for an animal to digest. The food item may actually turn foul in the animal's gut and regurgitation may result. If feeding is desired it is better to offer small items that leave little to no lump in the snake. Do not attempt to breed a female if she is skinny. She will not typically become reproductive if egg production would endanger her life.

The process basically works as follows: Healthy well-conditioned animals are triggered by environmental changes. Animals copulate multiple times over a few months during this cooling period. The female is further triggered by the mechanics of a courting and breeding male. These factors trigger follicle growth which are the immature unfertilized eggs. When the female breeds she retains sperm from the male which will later fertilize these ova once they are mature. As time passes the follicles mature to the approximate size (pecan- or walnut-sized). Lutinizing hormones elevate as the follicles mature and coincide with the development of viable follicles, which are now ready to be fertilized by retained sperm. During ovulation, the mature ova are released into the oviducts where they are fertilized by viable sperm.

Once this union has occured the female is known as "gravid". She is now pregnant with viable maturing eggs. The process of ovulation is known in the world of herpetoculture as "the lump". Ovulation visually appears as if the female had recently eaten a large meal and a noticeable swelling of her midsection with a very stiff feel to the animal's body. This exaggerated condition may only last for a day or two at most. This is the most important event to happen during the breeding process as without this we have no production in pythons and boas. After ovulation has occurred the eggs continue to grow and calcification of the shell ultimately occurs.

A healthy female is critical here. The eggs rob the female's body of stored fat and the bones of calcium. If the female is in poor condition she and the eggs may never make it through this process. This is nature's way of taking care of itself!

The female appears swollen as the egg follicles develop.

Keep all handling and activity to a minimum since this may have adverse results in viable egg production. Most males will lose all interest in a gravid female and breeding attempts should stop. She should be allowed to remain quiet and optimal basking temperatures should be provided. Keeping the female at a constant 85° F with a hot spot seems to satisfy the female's needs. A keeper should also provide a nesting box where she can hide. After ovulation we will see the female go into a pre egg-laying shed. This typically occurs 10 -14 days after ovulation. This shed now allows the breeder to predict egg laying; we generally see eggs laid 27 - 35 days after this shed. In some cases the female may take longer, up to 45 days after shed to lay. This may be due to cooler temperatures and slower egg development.

If a female ovulates she will not resorb her eggs. Breeders sometimes mistake a fat snake for an ovulating snake and wonder why they never get eggs. Once ovulation is observed for the first time it seems hard to mistake. Record shed and ovulation dates. This information will be very useful in understanding patterns of females or entire ball python collections. Do not attempt to feed a female after she has ovulated. She will not eat and the addition of a rodent to her environment will only be a source of stress.

What makes the female lay? The eggs are full-term, they have a shell, and a well yolked developing embryo. They now require more oxygen than the female can provide which triggers her to begin muscle contractions and to lay the eggs.

"The Lump" - ovulation, the point of conception.

Nesting female

As egg laying nears we will often add damp sphagnum or peat moss
to the female's nesting chamber. This imitates a natural nesting
situation for the female. A hide box or plastic storage box with an
entrance hole large enough for her to enter works well for this
purpose. Fill the chamber with moistened moss. It is better to use a
generous amount of nesting material since she will crowd herself into
the space and compress it to her liking. Do not locate the nest box on
or under the heat source, as the result may be that the female lays
the eggs in an area that is too hot and the eggs may die. It is better
to monitor the nest box temperature by placing a thermometer in the
nest box. Temperatures of 85° to 90° F are optimal. Digital thermometers with a probe are perfect for this as they allow the breeder
to note the temperature of the expecting female without disturbing
her. If the box is too cold or too hot she may fail to nest in a suitable
fashion and the clutch may be lost.

Females will often lay 27-35 days after her egg-laying preshed when
kept within her desired temperature range. Egg laying usually starts
in the late evening / early morning hours when it is dark and quiet.

Clutch size is typically five to six eggs but older females may average eight or better with clutches of 15 being remarkable. Small females may lay as few as two or three eggs their first time. Be careful when removing the female from her eggs as she will often resist your attempts at taking them and coil tightly around her clutch. Placing a towel over her head may reduce the stress to her and save the handler from being bitten. Unwrap her from the eggs, using both hands. It may help to have two people in this process. Do not rotate or drop the eggs. Remove them and set them into a container with media and move them into an incubator. After this, wash the female with dilute liquid dishwashing soap and water or a diluted Nolvasan® disinfectant solution. Make sure to rinse her off well. Clean the cage, remove the nest box, and replace the substrate. This removes the smell of the clutch and will help in getting her to feed again. If this is not done she may remain tightly coiled, twitching. Instincts are strong and she may remain this way for 60 days. This adds undue stress to her life.

Egg handling - Rule of thumb is not to rotate the eggs from their original position. As an egg develops it attaches blood vessels to the walls of the egg for oxygen absorption. If the egg is rotated there is a chance of the vessels pulling free and a resulting death of the embryo. I use a pencil to mark the tops of eggs and number them with large clutches. The lead graphite is harmless and works well.

Egg Viability

How to know if the egg is good: A fertile, viable egg is clean and white with a soft and leathery texture. Most fertile eggs will stick together and remain as a "clutch". Do not separate the eggs if this occurs since damage can lead to egg death. One method to authenticate viability is known as "candling"; in a dark room shine a bright flashlight on the egg and look for blood vessels inside. These blood vessels will appear as faint red lines and denote a fertile egg. Look carefully since it can be difficult to discern the blood vessels in some eggs. This technique will work on fresh eggs but waiting a few days will make the job easier since the blood vessels will increase in number and size as the embryo grows.

We may see eggs that appear white and perfect but are infertile due to lack of a breeding male or other unknown causes. These eggs will

be empty of blood vessels and will often start to turn bad within the first ten days of incubation. Yellow, soft uncalcified eggs, and small ova are known as "duds" and will not last the incubation process without rotting. These are the product of "bad breeders luck" and caused by many variables that cannot be explained with ease. When an egg is initially laid it may have a yellowish hue to it and will often change to white after it hardens, do not mistake this for a yellow unfertile egg.

Realize a snake egg is a flexible, absorbent housing for an embryo. The egg breathes and absorbs moisture from its immediate environment. Any chemicals or detergents can easily be absorbed into the egg, killing it. Imagine the surface of the egg to be layered with dots of calcium over a flexible skin, this protects it but makes it different than a hard chicken egg.

In the event a clutch is laid and there are any eggs that appear infertile remove the egg or eggs from the clutch if possible. We often see duds in the clutch that do not stick to viable eggs and these are easily separated from the good eggs. I sometimes encounter a clutch of good eggs with a single infertile egg stuck in the clutch. It can prove difficult to remove this egg from the perfect eggs without possible damage to other eggs. I carefully watch this egg during incubation. I typically note it beginning to rot and remove it from the clutch as it begins to break down. It is easier to peel this egg from the other eggs at this time, the important thing to remember is to remove it as it begins turning color.

If an an egg is allowed to rot it may have no effect on the other eggs or it may destroy attached eggs. Be careful during this process not to tear the shell of a good egg. The loss of a bad egg being peeled from

79

A proud and protective Bumble Bee mother.

a good egg is acceptable and does not destroy the integrity of the perfect egg.

Maternal Incubation

This is nature's way for python species and in the wild the eggs are dependent on the female to brood the clutch. The female will wrap herself in protective coils around the eggs, retaining heat and humidity. As she remains coiled she will occasionally twitch in a muscle contraction.

This was thought to release energy and add heat to the eggs. This theory has been disproven (Tamir Ellis energetic research on ball pythons) and the female does not have the ability to elevate the ambient temperature of the clutch beyond the environmental temperate. A brooding female may leave her clutch to bask and elevate her body temperature and then return to the eggs to raise the clutch temperature (G. Greer, pers. com.). Her body is the best thermostat and she will do her best to regulate the eggs to a perfect temperature. If they are too hot she will open her coils to cool the eggs. During this process she will not feed and in the wild may only rely on her water reserves, drink dew from her coils, or leave to drink and return to her clutch. In the wild the relative humidity in a burrow is extremely high,

Female coiled around a clutch of eggs.

providing an excellent environment for a brooding female. Some females may be lucky enough to gain entrance into a termite mound where the temperature and humidity is regulated at a constant by the resident termites. The conditions of the mound are perfect for egg incubation. This is also the favorite brooding chamber of the African Rock Python. It is a possibility that a female will use urine to add moisture to a clutch to prevent dehydration of the eggs.

If you have a female wrapped around eggs and do not have an incubator she may be left with the eggs until they hatch. While she is wrapped around the eggs, a keeper should increase cage humidity by spraying the surrounding substrate and female. Occasionally peek into her coils and look at the clutch to determine if they are drying out. If they are caving in, spray the female to add moisture. Using plenty of sphagnum moss in the nest area helps hold humidity. Maintain the cage temperature at 86 to 88° F using a thermostat located near her. Never leave the female to incubate eggs on a hot spot since this can kill the clutch.

An interesting point is that females will sometimes sense that an egg may be dead or infertile and push the egg free from her coils and fail to incubate it. I have tried to incubate these "roll out" eggs and find that these eggs almost always seem to fail regardless of what is done. I have put a "roll out" back into a female's maternal coils to later find that she has pinpointed the egg and pushed it from her coils. The ability for a female to do this protects a clutch from any defective eggs that may rot and spoil viable eggs within the clutch. As babies begin to hatch the female may nudge these eggs from her coils to allow the babies a chance to emerge from the egg. Maternally incubated clutches will often take longer to

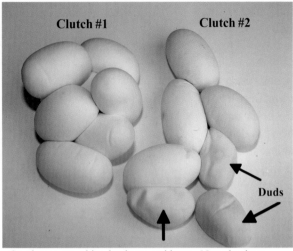

Good eggs are white, leathery, and large. Note the three infertile eggs, or duds, in Clutch #2.

hatch than artificial incubation due to the female's ambient temperature being lower than that of a controlled incubator.

Artificial Incubation

This is a critical point, please read and understand if you wish to have success. The eggs are contained typically in a Tupperware style vessel that has a few if not a single vent hole. This container is placed in the incubator. The incubator has a heating source that is controlled by a thermostat; rheostats on incubators are inappropriate since they are not self regulating and you can find accurate thermostats for an inexpensive price. The air around the egg chamber will change as the heat source fluctuates as the thermostat calls it. The egg chamber acts as a buffer and the temperatures inside change slowly. This is the key. If the temperature is immediately effective upon the eggs there will be a greater chance of development mishaps. The PROBE OF THE THERMOSTAT MUST BE PUT INTO THE EGG CHAMBER. Do not put it outside of the egg container since this will create unstable temps. DO NOT LOCATE THE EGG CONTAINER ON THE HEAT SOURCE as this can and will create hot spots that will damage the eggs. Raise the container up to prevent this potential problem. Use two digital thermometers that are first matched by locating the probes in a glass of water to

82

measure the readings. If they vary, use a normal accurate thermometer to decide the correct temp and then mark the deviation on each of the digital therms. They can then be used with a greater degree of accuracy in your incubator. I like using two; this ensures I will have no surprises down the road. I strongly suggest using a fan or two (depends upon incubator size and air path) within the incubator; the thermostat should control the fan. This

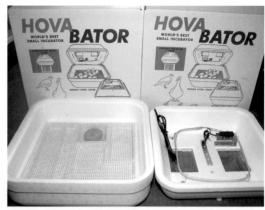

The Hovabator is a good, inexpensive incubator.

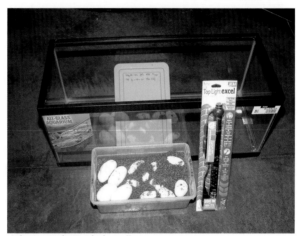

A homemade "tankubator".

ensures that the air surrounding the egg container has mixed well with the heat source and there will be less chance of hot spots. It is a wise choice to power up the incubator for at least 24 hours prior to the introduction of any eggs. This allows temperatures to stabilize and quality control the function of the incubator.

Egg Substrate

I suggest the use of the mineral Vermiculite. It is easy to obtain through and gardening store and very inexpensive. It holds water well and harbors no detrimental organisms at purchase. It comes in a number of granule sizes. I prefer the medium to coarse size particles. The fine-sized vermiculite tends to be messy but is still an effective egg medium. I also have used perlite for some lizard eggs, this can be tricky stuff to use since if the humidity is not kept properly it can and

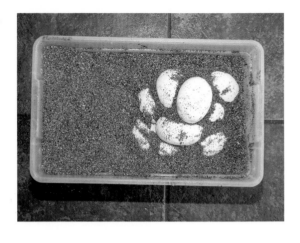

will draw moisture from the eggs that sit on it. I will not try to explain the incubating technique with this substance because I am not confident that I can explain it well enough for it to work. Peat moss can also be used, as well as a thick bed of sphagnum, but I would only use these substrates as a last resort. Remember, reptiles look for a place of high humidity and warmth to lay their eggs. If the substrate is too wet or too dry it will destroy the eggs.

Humidity - This is a critical point and varies from snake species to snake species. I will not discuss this in terms of a gauge; I never use one but depend on reading the eggs and the level of moisture within the egg chamber. We are typically thinking of levels of 90-100% ambient humidity. We often tend to go overboard on the moisture content that we provide when first attempting to incubate python eggs. General rule of thumb is to add small amounts of water to the vermiculite as you mix it. Make sure it is mixed well. Typically add enough water to clump the vermiculite slightly when you squeeze it into a clump. No water should come out and it should flake apart easily. A simple ratio is two parts vermiculite and one part water by weight.

After the eggs have set up in a day or so note the amount of water condensation within the container and its lid. It should be slight if at all, not dripping. A wet egg box will kill the eggs, they will turn green, smell and mold up. Eggs do not have a method of dealing with too much moisture. The eggs will absorb whatever they are in contact with. IMPORTANT - it is easier to save an egg that has dried out a bit from low humidity than to save one that has been exposed to too much. Don't go overboard. A white egg that is dimpled or slightly caved in is accept-able and can easily be fixed by wetting

Note the healthy baby in the foreground and the smaller head of the premature baby hatching behind it.

some of the medium and putting it over the eggs for a day or two. A snake egg that appears a bit dimpled is nothing to worry about. Some eggs may fill out while others look a bit caved in. A living healthy egg will absorb the extra direct moisture. If the eggs are turning foul, moldy, green, yellow or blue this is a dead or dying egg. This is also may be a good indication that it is too moist within the egg container. Remove all bad eggs whenever possible, do not damage an attached egg by the removal of a bad one. Many eggs, if healthy and provided the proper environment, will exist attached to a shriveled dead egg. If they go moldy and turn colors they will often damage the attached egg and are typically easy to remove as they decay! If this occurs you may want to rethink if the eggs are too wet. I tend to lay down a thick bed of vermiculite, at least three inches and then put the eggs on top of it adding more medium covering the clutch 2/3'rds of the way. The trick is to keep the humidity level

The slicing open of the egg is the first stage of hatching.

85

constant and protect the eggs from drying out or having water droplets land on them.

Air – I use a few holes that are 1/8 – 1/4" drilled or melted through the egg container. That is all of the air they will need. Do not worry about eggs being covered by a few inches of vermiculite,

A baby begins to breathe and metabolize its yolk.

they still get the oxygen they need. At about day 50 I will uncover the clutch and start watching the eggs progress.

Egg Development

After an egg is laid, it grows in mass and draws its moisture from its environment and nourishment from its yolk. We notice that snake eggs will often cause the egg chamber to sweat as they prepare to hatch. This may start at day 48 or later. They are warming up! They are actually creating a bit of their own heat that may be several degrees in larger clutches. At some point in the incubation process large clutches may create too much heat and actually cause embryo death and deformities. Watch out for this on large clutches, check your temps as time passes. I generally incubate all python eggs at 90° F but it seems a bit wiser to incubate large clutches at lower temps such as 88° F. A slightly lower incubation temperature may allow for some temperature deviation in a home built incubator; 88° F is a safe base temperature.

Close to hatch - The box begins to sweat with increasing humidity as the developing babies start to metabolize their yolk. They now have greater demands and actually generate a bit of their own heat causing the egg container to heat up. The egg's shell becomes soft or brittle as the animal releases enzymes to break down the shell. This enables the baby to cut or break free from its shell.

Baby snakes have an "egg tooth" located on the tip of their nose which allows them to score and cut the inside surface of the egg. With pythons I often separate the eggs from each other a few days before they are due to hatch, this prevents snakes from slitting into another egg and possibly drowning. This is generally done around day 53 @ 88° F. The eggs are easier to separate at this point and can be done with relative safety if care is taken and the eggs are not rotated. Gently peel the eggs apart if you choose to do this. If you are unsure it is better to leave the clutch alone.

Understanding Your Ball Python 101

Corey Woods

In captivity, snakes have needs. As keepers we must first meet the needs of the snake before we can expect to enjoy what makes it unique to us. Reptiles are cold-blooded and directly depend on their environment for heat. This heat allows the animal to maintain temperatures that allow proper digestion and growth, and allows the immune system to function. If we fail to provide the proper temperature range we will not provide a critical basic requirement that allows the animal to function. The animal may live for a time but weaken and succumb to disease or starvation without proper temperatures.

A ball python's natural instinct is to be secretive and most active at night, making it nocturnal. A snake of such modest size would not last long in the African bush if it exposed itself to predators during the day on a regular basis. They have minimal forms of defense and have survived well by being secretive and living much of the time in underground haunts. In captivity, the animal should have a day period and a night period where it feels safe to venture from its artificial burrow. If we fail to provide what the snake feels as a safe and secure environment it may never "settle in" and may remain nervous and uncomfortable. This does not translate into a healthy situation since the animal may fail to thrive. The keeper must provide hiding locations and keep the animal in a reasonably quiet location. Keeping the ball python in an area of heavy foot traffic and the constant exposure to disruption from people and pets should be avoided. Snakes learn, but it takes time for the animal to understand that people are not predators. Once you have gained the animal's trust through time and gentle handling, it will often learn to accept human contact and the occasional interruption of its daily life. Some ball pythons even seem to enjoy the human activity and are very curious to explore their environment. These are well-acclimated animals that have learned we do not wish to eat them, we have become part of their environment, and we do not pose a threat.

Interpreting your ball python's behavior

Snakes live their lives in a few basic modes. Gaining a basic understanding of these modes will help you as a keeper to "read" your snake, better allowing you to meet the animal's needs.

Sleeping

Snakes will lay motionless with their pupil barely dilated to prevent excessive light from entering the eyes. Remember, they do not have eyelids. Snakes will spend much of the day sleeping and waiting to ambush prey. A snake can immediately move from sleeping to attacking a prey item. This is nature's way of ensuring optimal use of the event. . . it may be quite some time before another opportunity comes along. The keeper must realize that a snake may occasionally bite if this is not understood. Example: You pet your cat and then go and try to pick up your sleeping snake. The snake has been waiting all day with a hair trigger. Sudden movement, the smell of fur, and a warm object may initiate an attempt to secure prey. The excited snake snags the keeper's hand and a startling event occurs. The snake acted on instinct and the keeper did not practice a responsible approach. Washing your hands after touching anything furry may be a good precaution, and waking the snake up enough to allow it to go into thinking mode is advised. This mode is when the snake actually investigates its environment, taking in smells, heat signatures, and all the activity it can sense. Watch the snake, long tongue flicks and inquisitive meandering are a definite sign of a content and thinking snake. In this mode the snake is unlikely to mistake you as a potential food item and this is the mode we enjoy the most.

My personal thoughts are that snakes do recognize their keepers given enough time to learn who you are and how the two of you interact. Some snakes may be nervous when handled by a stranger and may appear spastic; this is a snake that is afraid and uncomfortable with the situation. When a snake feels that it may fall or it is being mishandled, it may become agitated and quick moving. At this point it may be inclined to bite as it tries to defend itself. This is defensive behavior. This is not the snake being mean. Nature equipped this little python with many short, needle-like teeth that assure the animal of being noticed if it chooses to bite. The majority of ball pythons are unlikely to bite unless great harm is feared. Occasionally we find the lemon in the group. I have seen outwardly aggressive ball pythons that may even go out of their way to snap at me. These snakes are unusually nervous and basically fear the world is out to get them. They are biting out of excessive fear, not because they are mean. Mean is a human emotion and serves no purpose in the animal kingdom.

Depression

I also believe some snakes may act depressed when things are not correct in their environment. These snakes seem to become inactive and secretive. This may occur when the cage is located in the path of heavy traffic and the snake never feels secure. Over time this effect can lead to the demise of an otherwise healthy ball python. There are a host of things that can cause this effect, so it is important to understand the basic requirements of the animal and then add a good dose of common sense.

Imagine being placed in a beautiful home without a phone. Every time you go outside of your house there is a giant Godzilla looking at you, so you run back inside and hide. The Godzilla is very excited to see you so he picks up your house and pulls you out and looks you over. After a time the Godzilla loses interest in you and places you back in your yard and puts your house down. Godzilla did not actually hurt you, but he is still Godzilla. At this point he is not to be trusted. You are frequented by Godzilla, who provides you with plenty of food and water. The rumbles of Godzilla are felt with frequency. You are very nervous of this situation. At any moment Godzilla could demand your presence and awaken you, removing you from your home. Sometimes Godzilla has other monster friends that also play with you but never hurt you. It is a scary experience and it takes time to trust Godzilla. At first the experience may have terrified you and you did not feel comfortable, but you learned that Godzilla did not harm you. Over time you may even feel comfortable with your Godzilla.

Snakes need time to settle in, to understand their surroundings, and to trust the human / snake interaction factor.

Tips on being a successful snake keeper:

Be Educated

Be Observant

Be Proactive
Be Reasonable

Be Open to Advice!

Be a problem solver – don't be afraid to think!

Research, research, research! There are books and an internet full of good information, but watch out for "self-appointed experts" in on-line forums.

Join a herpetological society in your area.

Visit reptile expos and specialty shops and talk to established breeders.

Enjoy your animals!

PHOTO GALLERY

Albino. Photo by Kevin McCurley. Animal by NERD.

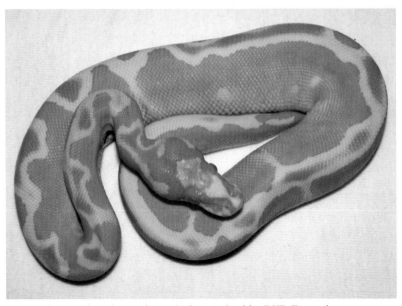

Albino Clown. Photo by Kevin McCurley. Animal by BHB Enterprises.

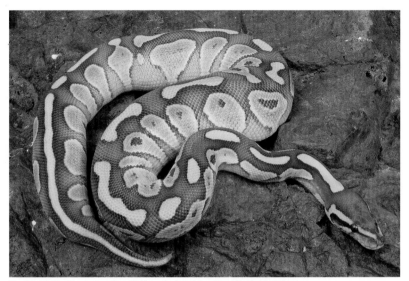

Butter Ball. Photo by Jay Vella. Animal by Reptile Industries.

Caramel Glow. Photo by Kevin McCurley. Animal by NERD.

Clown. Photo by Kevin McCurley. Animal by NERD.

Pastel Clown. Photo by Kevin McCurley. Animal by BHB Enterprises.

Coral Glow. Photo by Kara Glasgow. Animal by NERD.

Desert Ghost. Photo by Kevin McCurley. Animal by NERD.

Hypomelanistic / Ghost. Photo by Kevin McCurley. Animal by NERD.

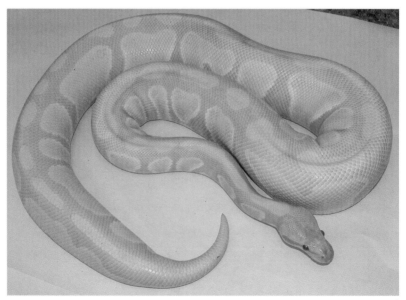

Lavender Albino. Photo by Kevin McCurley. Animal by NERD.

Blue-eyed Leucistic. Photo by Ralph Davis. Animal by RDR.

Lemon Pastel - Super. Photo by Kevin McCurley. Animal by NERD.

Pied. Photo by Kevin McCurley. Animal by NERD.

Pinstripe. Photo by Rich Crowley. Animal by Chicago Reptile House.

98

Spider. Photo by Kevin McCurley. Animal by NERD.

Ghost Spider / Honey Bee. Photo by Kevin McCurley. Animal by NERD.

Lemon Bumblebee. Photo by Kevin McCurley. Animal by NERD.

Killer Bee / Spider Super Pastel. Photo by Kevin McCurley. Animal by NERD.

SUGGESTED READING

Armstrong, M. 1979. Induced feeding of royal python. *The Herptile*, 4(3): 9–10.

Barker D. and T.Barker. 1995. The mechanics of python reproduction. *The Vivarium* 6(5):30-33.

Barker, D., and T. Barker. 1999. The belle of the ball. *Reptiles*, 7(9): 48–65.

Barker, D., and T. Barker. 1996. Pythons and boas in your home. *Reptiles Annual 1996*: 32–47.

Bartlett, R. D. 2000. Ball Pythons (Reptile Keepers Series). Barrons publishing. Hauppauge, NY.

Broghammer, S. 2004. Ball Pythons: Habitat, Care, and Breeding (Revised & Expanded Edition). M & S Verlag. Germany.

Coote, J. G. 1996. Ball Pythons: Their Captive Husbandry and Reproduction. Practical Python Publications. Nottingham, UK.

De Vosjoli, P. 1990. The General Care and Maintenance of Ball Pythons. Advanced Vivarium Systems. Mission Viejo, CA.

De Vosjoli, P. 2004. *The Art of Keeping Snakes*. Advanced Vivarium Systems, Lakeside, California.

Klingenberg, R. J. 1993. *Understanding Reptile Parasites*. Advanced Vivarium Systems, Lakeside.

McCurley, K. 2005. *The Complete Ball Python: A Comprehensive Guide to Care, Breeding, and Mutations*. ECO Herp. Publ. & Dist. Lansing, MI.

Peterson K. 1993. Husbandry and breeding of ball pythons (*Python regius*). The Vivarium 5(1):18-27.

Van Mierop, L. H. S., and E. L. Bessette. 1981. Reproduction of the ball python, *Python regius*, in captivity. *Herpetological Review*, 12(1) 20–22.

Wagner E. 1997. Ask the breeder: Ball python breeding strategy. Reptiles 5(8):89.

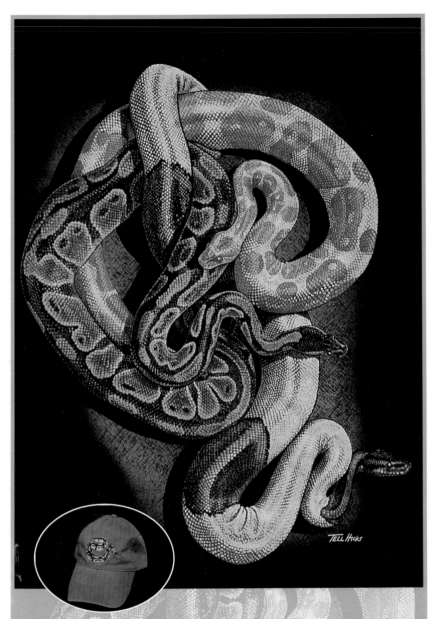